SOFT SKILLS FOR LEADERS

Other Titles by Wanda S. Maulding Green and Edward E. Leonard

A Field Book for Higher Education Leaders: Improving Your Leadership Intelligence (Rowman & Littlefield Publishers, January, 2018)

Improving Your Leadership Intelligence: A Field Book for K–12 Leaders (Rowman & Littlefield Publishers, September, 2017)

Leadership Intelligence: Navigating to Your True North (Rowman & Littlefield Publishers, September, 2016)

The Soft Skills of Leadership: Navigating with Confidence and Humility, 2nd Edition (Rowman & Littlefield Publishers, November, 2019)

Growing Your Leadership: Scenarios from Practicing K–12 Principals, Volume 2 (Rowman & Littlefield Publishers, December, 2019)

SOFT SKILLS FOR LEADERS

SCENARIOS FROM HIGHER EDUCATION ADMINISTRATORS, VOLUME 2

Wanda S. Maulding Green
and Edward E. Leonard

ROWMAN & LITTLEFIELD
Lanham • Boulder • New York • London

Published by Rowman & Littlefield
An imprint of The Rowman & Littlefield Publishing Group, Inc.
4501 Forbes Boulevard, Suite 200, Lanham, Maryland 20706
www.rowman.com

6 Tinworth Street, London SE11 5AL, United Kingdom

British Library Cataloguing in Publication Information Available

Library of Congress Cataloging-in-Publication Data Available

Library of Congress Control Number: 2019953205

ISBN: 978-1-4758-4961-5 (pbk. : alk. paper)
ISBN: 978-1-4758-4962-2 (electronic)

♾™ The paper used in this publication meets the minimum requirements of American National Standard for Information Sciences—Permanence of Paper for Printed Library Materials, ANSI/ NISO Z39.48–1992.

CONTENTS

PREFACE

In preparing to compose a new preface for this second volume of *Soft Skills for Leaders: Scenarios from Higher Education Administrators, Volume 2,* the original preface was reread numerous times. The end result of those readings was that we still felt that the preface captured the essence of what we wanted to say with some additions based on current commentary and research. Those additions are addressed in the new part of the preface contained in the third paragraph.

One of the key points in *The Soft Skills of Leadership: Navigating with Confidence and Humility*[1] is that the soft skills that comprise the major leader acumen *imperatives* of credibility, competence, inspirational ability, vision, and emotional intelligence/soft skills can be learned. Leaders, aspiring leaders, or anyone who wishes to build their leader acumen, with proper exposure and practice, can learn new skills or enhance skills they already possess. Learning or enhancing skills builds a leader's adaptive capacity. In *Geeks and Geezers: How Era, Values, and Defining Moments Shape Leaders*, Warren Bennis and Robert Thomas shared as follows:

> To the extent that any single quality determines success, that quality is adaptive capacity. . . . When we look at who becomes a leader, we see enormous variance in IQ, birth order, family wealth, family stability, level of education, ethnicity, race, and gender. Certainly, these factors cannot be dismissed entirely. But in studying both very young and older leaders, we found over and over again that much more important than a person's measured intelligence—to take just one factor—was his or her ability to transcend the limits that a particular IQ might impose. In the case of intelligence, this includes avoiding the trap of seeing oneself as highly intelligent, hopelessly average, or below average to the exclusion of other, more useful self-definitions. We emphatically agree with Ford's Elizabeth Kao that "everyone has their own wall to climb." And we believe that both the willingness to climb those walls and the ability to find ways to do so are the real measure of a leader.[2]

Bennis and Thomas go on to say that leaders "learn important lessons, including new skills that allow them to move on to new levels of achievement and new levels of learning. This ongoing process of challenge, adaptation, and learning prepares the individual for the next crucible, where the process is repeated. Whenever significant new problems are encountered and dealt with adaptively, new levels of competence are achieved, better preparing the individual for the next challenge."[3]

Summarizing the concept of adaptive capacity in later writing, Bennis reemphasized the importance of adaptive capacity saying "the ruling quality of leaders, adaptive capacity, is what allows true leaders to make the nimble decisions that bring success."[4] Making correct decisions is based on three premises: knowledge of a given situation, technical (hard/competency-based) skills, and (soft) people skills. Knowledge of events will vary from situation to situation but a leader cannot succeed without the people skills that allow him or her to fully utilize his or her technical skills. It is the recognition of the importance of acquiring the technical and people skills and moving to acquire and/ or enhance those skills as new discoveries or innovations occur or when new strategies develop that is the cornerstone of building leader acumen that allows a leader's adaptive capacity to flourish.

Current commentary and research continue to emphasize the importance of adaptive capacity or the ability to accommodate change and expand that concept to include the ability of an organization to be adaptive. John Chambers, the chief executive officer of CISCO, a leading worldwide technology firm, has this to say about adaptive capacity or the ability to accommodate change: "I think now most CEOs would agree. If they don't change, they get left behind." He further contends that "she or he has to think much more outside the box. They have to reinvent themselves. They have to reinvent their company."[5] Leaders must adapt and so must the organization they lead. According to Uhl-Bien and Arena (2018), "Leadership for organizational adaptability calls for scholars and practitioners to recognize organizational adaptability as an important organizational outcome, and enabling leadership (i.e., enabling the adaptive process through adaptive space) as a critical form of leadership for adaptive organizations."

And that enabling leadership "addresses how leaders can position organizations and the people within them to be adaptive in the face of complex challenges."[6] Moreover, Uhl-Bien and Arena share that "organizations and those within them (need) to be flexible, agile and adaptive in response to changes associated with a volatile and often unpredictable world."[7] The CEO Chambers and the researchers Uhl-Bien and Arena come to the same conclusion as Bennis and Thomas that adaptive capacity is vital to individual and organizational success.

Soft Skills for Leaders: Scenarios from Higher Education Administrators, Volume 2 takes the readers through a series of situational judgment tests or SJTs that address the soft people skill areas that lead to success. The SJTs are drawn from real-life experiences and are testament to the challenges, large and small, that a leader faces and the leader acumen and adaptive capacity a leader must exercise to make correct decisions.

However, there is one difference between the SJTs in volumes 1 and 2. The authors (Maulding Green and Leonard) developed the SJTs in volume 1 from their own individual experiences. The SJTs in volume 2 combine additional SJTs from Maulding Green and Leonard with SJTs from higher education practitioners who are either still active in the field or recently retired. Developing or enhancing your leader acumen and adaptive capacity and thereby your ability to make proper decisions is a foundational leadership ability. *Soft Skills for Leaders: Scenarios from Higher Education Administrators, Volume 2* takes you on a leadership development journey. It is a leadership world directed at educating each student. As Catherine Bond Hill, president of Vassar College, shared in her 2010 address to the Vassar spring convocation:[8]

> What could better capture the ideal of the education that we've aspired to provide? It is an education that is less about defining a path, rather very much an education that allows one to choose paths—the open road. It is an education that creates options—life-long options—through both having nurtured a robust curiosity and having developed the tools necessary to satisfy that curiosity. So, you have options . . . leading wherever you choose, the world before you.

INTRODUCTION

THE CONCEPT OF LEADER ACUMEN

Leader Acumen is defined as "a construct that represents the level of leadership capacity an individual possesses at any given time. It addresses the leadership imperatives of individuals including: credibility, competence, ability to inspire, vision, and emotional intelligence."[9] Each of these leadership imperatives is subdivided into knowledge, skills, and dispositions, as shown in the following table. Each of the imperative subscale items lend themselves to defining the major category.

Leader Acumen Imperatives				
Credibility *In 500 feet, stay right*	*Competence* *Recalculating*	*Inspiration* *Satellite reception lost*	*Vision* *You have arrived at your destination*	*Emotional Intelligence* *Route guidance suggested*
Ethics or personal accountability	Discernibility	Enthusiastic	Commitment	Resilience
Honesty	Perception	Energetic	Sense of direction	Communication and listening
Responsibility	Conflict resolution skills	Passionate	Professionalism	Happiness
Trust	Problem-solving and decision-making Skills	Optimistic	Decisive	Personality traits
Integrity	Relationship building	Genuine	Work ethic	Sense of humor
Sincerity	Planning and implementation	Courageous	Concern for the future	Assertiveness
	Assessment and Evaluation			Flexibility
				Empathy/ interpersonal interactions

Source: Maulding Green and Leonard (2016, p. 19)

Accompanying *The Soft Skills of Leadership: Navigating with Confidence and Humility* is the Leader Acumen assessment. It includes the subscale items listed in the earlier table that the LSI assessment is designed to measure. Ideally, the best starting point for using this handbook is to take the LSI assessment, if you have not yet done so. The assessment is available free of charge online at https://www.leadershipimprinting. com/.

This is a self-assessment and it is vitally important that you are absolutely candid in your responses. The results of the assessment will give you a snapshot of your leadership capacity. It is important for the test taker to acknowledge, however, that the assessment is a fluid one. You may take it today after a great day at work and reveal a higher score than you might, for instance, if taken when you have had many difficult days as a leader.

For a broader look at your leadership capacity, the authors suggest that you conduct a 360-evaluation (alternately referred to as a CIRCLE assessment) by having people you work with, those who evaluate you, or those who work *for* you complete the survey. Conducting a 360-assessment to accompany your self-assessment will provide you with a measure of the match or congruence of your view of your leadership capacity with the view of others directly associated with you as a leader or aspiring leader. You may do this by inquiring on the website via the "Contact Us" page at https://www.leadershipim printing.com/. Based on the results of your self-assessment and/or your 360-assessment, you are ready to work through the book *Soft Skills for Leaders: Scenarios from Higher Education Administrators, Volume 2.*

However, taking the assessment is not required to make good use of the field book. The scenarios provided in the field book are a source from which to develop insight into and familiarity with the real-life situations with which higher education leaders or leaders in general deal. Most of the events described in the field manual could and do happen to any leader (perhaps in a slightly different context). Leaders share many commonalities in terms of the issues with which they must deal, especially the soft-skill/ people-related issues.

HOW TO USE THE FIELD BOOK INDIVIDUALLY

Use of the field book is straightforward and simple. There are thirty-four scenarios based on the five imperatives of leader acumen. Leader Acumen All of the scenarios are higher education-based but are potentially adaptive to all leadership situations.

Select a scenario. Read the scenario carefully. Think about the situation described and the possible solutions. Jot down in the space provided the solution you think would lead to the best outcome for the scenario. Then jot down a rationale for your solution.

After you have completed this part of the activity, turn to the end of the chapter where the *Authors' Options* are located. Read the options carefully and choose a best response from those listed. (Note, each scenario lists a final option that is blank. If you believe your solution is better than those provided by the authors, you should pencil your solution in at this time.)

With your solution and rationale in hand and your choice from the *Authors' Options* list (or your own solution), turn to the section of the field book titled *Authors' Solutions* for SJTs to see the authors' solution* to the SJT (these are listed by chapter and scenario). Compare your solution and rationale to the *Authors' Solutions*. Close alignment of your solution and rationale with that provided suggests a well-honed sense of analysis of the situation. It is important to realize, though, that while some solutions and the accompanying rationale are better than others, there is often more than one acceptable way to resolve an issue/situation.

As a last step to gain further insight, the authors encourage you to read the complementary reading from *The Soft Skills of Leadership: Navigating with Confidence and Humility* and the relevant, contemporary selected related readings listed at the end of each scenario. Follow this same cycle as you read/work through the field manual.

HOW TO USE THE FIELD BOOK WITH GROUPS OR INSTRUCTIONALLY

Using the field book as an instructional tool follows the same general pattern as for individual use with some differences. Divide the class into small groups. Provide each group with an SJT scenario. Instruct the group members to read the scenario carefully, think about the situation described and the possible solutions, and jot down individually in the space provided how they would respond to the scenario. Then jot down a rationale for the solution.

After each individual has completed this part of the activity, the facilitator should direct the groups to the end of the chapter where the *Authors' Options* are located. Individually, again, the class members should choose a best response from those listed. (Note, each scenario lists a final option that is blank. If the student believes his or her solution is better than those provided by the authors, he or she should pencil it in at this time.)

Next, time should be allowed within the small groups to share their choices and come to group consensus on the best solution. Time should also be allowed for discussion and dialogue regarding the rationale for the individual choices. (Prior to class, instructors should prepare answer-sharing cards to be utilized for this part of the activity. See Appendix A, for an example.) After ample small group discussion time has been given, the instructor should ask the small groups to *raise the card* with the letter of the solution they have chosen.

The instructor should then guide the large group instruction regarding the choices the small groups have made with ensuing dialogue. All of this rich discourse is intended to help *grow* participants "adaptive capacity" for leadership. Additionally, the instructor may choose to share the *Authors' Solutions* with rationale along with rationale for rejection of the other choices. Repeat the process for each SJT scenario.

Whether used individually or in a group setting, the use of SJTs adds an element of realism to the concepts presented. SJTs also allow the readers to utilize their analytic skills and judgment in synthesizing a solution and rationale. Each of these is needed in a leadership situation as any decision can and, in all likelihood, will be examined and criticized and a leader must be able to defend his or her decisions.

Finally, to fully solidify the learning from the class, the complementary reading from *The Soft Skills of Leadership: Navigating with Confidence and Humility* is listed at the end. Additionally, relevant, contemporary selected related readings are presented at the end of each scenario to solidify the learning gained through practice.

HEADED IN THE RIGHT DIRECTION?

The conceptual model for *Leader Acumen* is a Global Positioning System (GPS). With that framework in mind, there are many "directions" you might take to get to a final destination. As such, you may review your *Leader Acumen Assessment* and determine to work on the area where your score is lowest. That is fine. For example, you might skip over to the chapter with VISION-growing scenarios if that works best for you. The field book was designed for use individually if desired.

If you are an instructor, working with a class, the quickest route to your destination might be to work through from the beginning to the end. On the other hand, you might want to vary the scenarios to accommodate everyone in your class, rather than going through each topic before moving to the next. For you, getting to your destination might include waypoints along the route.

For all, the main thing to remember is that there are many ways to get to a specific destination. There is more than one correct way to solve a problem, and the quickest route to a solution may not always be the wisest. As you work through the scenarios, you will gain confidence in your navigational skills and become a better leader along the way.

SITUATIONAL JUDGMENT TESTS

Situational judgment tests (SJTs) are assessments where the test taker is presented with a real or hypothetical situation and is then asked to select the most appropriate response to that scenario. SJTs have been around since the early 1920s. They have been used for garnering feedback of those from managerial positions in the workplace to decision-making ability in the military.[10] Over the years, they have proved to be good predictors of job performance. The authors believe SJTs are a good tool to use, especially for a field book of the nature of this one because as McDaniel and Whetzel put it, they (SJTs):

- have low adverse impact,
- assess soft skills,
- have good acceptance by applicants,
- assess job-related skills not tapped by other measures, and
- assess "non-academic, practical intelligence."[11]

With those considerations in mind, the SJT is an excellent tool to use when growing one's skillset in *Leader Acumen*. As earlier stated, the typical format of a SJT is for a brief scenario to be shared with the learner. Of course, this sharing may be done via video clip, live via role-play, or in a written form. After the students acknowledge the situation, typically, they are given multiple-choice responses to review and then select from. In this field book, an additional step is added.

Prior to exposure to the authors' multiple-choice answer options, the student is allowed to pen his or her own brief response to the scenario. This is done to allow the opportunity for rapid processing of *typical* thought processes: "What would I do in this situation without suggestion from others?" It allows the readers to reflect on his or her own "gut level" response before being guided. This step, the internalization of an individual's usual/typical response, is critical in the growth aspect of this learning process.

It is important, then, for the readers to respond in the provided space as quickly and as honestly as possible. The readers should not be asking, "How *should* I respond" but rather "How have I responded to a similar problem in the past" or even "What do I think is the best way to respond?"

For the classroom teacher, instructor, or workshop facilitator, SJTs have the best outcomes when the situation is presented to an individual (or group of individuals) via "live" mechanisms, that is, role-play, video cast, or podcast. However, they are still effective when shared only in written form. Traditionally, SJTs come in a variety of formats and responding mechanisms. Some are developed requiring the participants to rank order the stated options; others ask the participants to give only the *best* answer, yet others call for the *unacceptable* responses. For the most part, the SJTs included in this field book ask for the participant to give the best response.

Additionally, the authors have (at the end of the book) given the *Authors' Solutions* to the SJTs (whether correct or incorrect) a best response with a rationale for that decision, and, similarly, have given rationales for the other choice options. The most important takeaway for these exercises is to help the readers hear a range of potential responses to a situation and most importantly, for the participants, over time, to become reflective learners.

The richness of these assessments comes from the facilitation of an invested leader into and through individual, small-group, and large-group sharing and interaction. It is through these mechanisms that the best and most rapid learning can take place. Supporting readings from the companion book, *The Soft Skills of Leadership: Navigating with Confidence and Humility,* follow each scenario but should not preempt the SJT itself. Additionally, selected relevant, contemporary related readings are presented at the end of each scenario to solidify the learning gained through practice.

SJTs have been selected as the primary tool to help a student grow his or her own *Leader Acumen.* These learnings, as shared in *The Soft Skills of Leadership: Navigating with Confidence and Humility,* take time and repetitive activity to establish as norms as they are acquired in the most basal or primary parts of our brains.

1

LESSONS ON CREDIBILITY

One of the things that people notice about a leader, possibly more than any other thing a leader does, is the extent to which his or her actions are consistent with his or her articulated position. Followers are asking and answering (to their own satisfaction) a vital question about the leader. Does he or she say what he or she means and support that with his or her actions? The answer to that question defines the credibility of the leader.

The scenarios in this chapter are, in one way or another, related to a leader's credibility. If your Leader Acumen assessment scores indicate this as an area for needed growth, you should work through the scenarios with a couple of things in mind. First, as you work through the scenarios in the chapter, take particular note of the *Authors' Options* to each problem at the end of each chapter of SJTs. In working through the scenarios and reviewing the *Authors' Options*, one of two things will happen. You will find disparity between your responses and the authors, or you might, indeed, find that your responses coincide with the authors' (see Appendix B for a graphic representation). Next, reflect on the information you gained from the LSI assessment. If you acknowledge that Credibility is an area for growth based on the assessment, ask yourself if this was based on your Self-assessment, the Circle assessment, or both.

If either or both assessments (the Self or Circle) indicate that you have room for improvement in the area of leader Credibility *and* you are also finding disparity in yours and the *Authors' Options*, chances are you will find growth via working through these exercises and accompanying readings. However, be reminded, this will not happen overnight. Growing your Leader Acumen is a worthy endeavor but is a painstakingly time-consuming undertaking. It requires rewiring of your thought processes regarding learnings that are very much ingrained into your most innate thought processes and this takes time (see Appendix B for a graphic representation).

On the other hand, if you find your solutions and the solutions offered in the *Authors' Options* coincide highly, yet your Self score is lower than the means for the group shown at the end of your assessment for Credibility, one of two things is happening. Either you are lacking in self-confidence, yet your decision-making is solid, or perhaps you are somewhat overconfident but nonetheless making good decisions. If the first is the case, working through the scenarios should enhance your self-confidence. The second option (overconfidence) is the one to be most wary of. Leaders in this category many times find themselves derailed as leaders, even though they generally are good decision makers. Working through the scenarios should help in instilling the idea that there is more than one acceptable solution to most problem/issues and thus lessen one potential major consequence of overconfidence, feeling that you have the only viable solution.

If you opt to have a Circle/360-assessment done and find that your solutions and the solutions offered in the *Authors' Options* coincide highly, yet your Circle scores are outside the standard deviation (available from the LEAD team when a Circle/360-assessment is done) LEA for Credibility, it is possible that a different set of problems is occurring. Either you are selecting the course of action you believe is best for the scenario, yet in reality you would not implement it, or the problem may be one of *perception*. It is much more likely that it is the former. Only in rare instances would the latter be the case. However, we insert it here for thought because, on occasion, it is the case. And, as the old saying goes, perception is reality.

Perhaps you are indeed highly credible yet *perception* is the issue for your low scores in Credibility. This could be a case of projection. For example, you may not "look" credible and perhaps for legitimate reasons. You will recall from the chapter on credibility in *The Soft Skills of Leadership: Navigating with Confidence and Humility* (2nd edition), that mention was made of how "what you wear" infers or projects an image. Such could be the case in this instance.

Finally, improving your Leader Acumen and "adaptive capacity," as stated in the preface, is a process. As you will recall, the notion of Leader Acumen is predicated on the theory that there is a genetic predisposition toward leadership.

As Marquis and Tilscik[1] so aptly noted, imprinting may take place, during brief sensitive periods of high susceptibility during the formative process, during the teachable moment or another yet different time of susceptibility, and that imprints once established are persistent.

The lessons in this book are to be utilized to grow Leader Acumen in this third way— over the long, repetitive process. To that end and to truly be imprinted with any of the competencies, actions for building the various skillsets may be found in Appendix C.

True Credibility is only gained by congruence of words and actions.

CLINICAL TRIALS AND TRIBULATIONS

You are the associate dean and it is your charge to ensure that students are treated fairly and are held to high academic standards. It is late in the semester, and late on one of the last Fridays of the term, you receive a phone call from an upset student. The student tells you, "I was dismissed from my program today but have been in the hospital for two weeks. My instructor told me that I had missed too much of my clinical coursework and dismissed me from the program." The student provides additional details revealing two hospitalizations in the semester with the most recent being the longest time period.

Through your conversation you learn that the student is on scholarship with the Saudi Arabian government paying the tuition. The student is concerned that returning home would be required due to the dismissal. You find it odd that the student is more concerned about having to go home than the actual dismissal. You ask if the student has medical documentation and the student confirms such stating it had been provided directly to the instructor. You tell the student the university has policies to protect students with documented medical excuses and that you will investigate and call back early in the new week.

You then walk down to talk with the program's department chair. When you arrive in the department, you learn the chair has left for the day. You then decide to approach the instructor to learn his side of the story. The instructor confirms that the student had missed too many days of clinical rotations, so he was suspended, as had been done with other students in the past.

You ask, "Was the student able to provide you with medical documentation of illness?" He confirms that the student had provided documentation of illness but that there was nothing he could do to help and as such suspended him. You remind the instructor of the policy that requires students with medical documentation be allowed to make up missed work. Without acknowledgment of your remark, he states that the program faculty have plans to discuss the student's suspension and likely dismissal on Monday. He seems unconcerned that the student's visa would be revoked requiring he go home upon dismissal.

You return to your office and email the student (and copy the department chair). In the email, you confirm having started an investigation into the situation and your understanding that program faculty will be discussing this in the new week. You instruct the student to provide the medical documentation via email to the Dean of Students and/or Students with Disabilities Office so that they may confirm the illness with the instructor per institutional policy.

The student responds to you and provides copies of all medical documentation later that evening. The student also shares that he was instructed not to attend the clinical rotation on Monday due to the dismissal. As you open the medical documentation you see that the student's gender is marked as female. Throughout the situation you had thought the student was male. The instructor referred to the student as "he."

On Monday, you approach the department chair in person regarding the situation. The chair reveals that the student is "a transgender" and dresses as a woman. He states that "he" is from Saudi Arabia and has missed a great deal of class this term. The chair believes the absences are due to gender-related surgeries even though the medical documentation indicates a specific illness. The department chair says that it is too much work for the instructor to provide make-up clinical rotations by the end of the term and so dismissal is the appropriate action.

The pieces come together and you realize the medical documentation reflects the student's current and preferred gender; however, the faculty members in the department have not recognized this and continue to call the student "he." Additionally, the student is from a country that would not be accepting of a person born male transitioning to female.

What will you do?

_____

_____

_____

_____

_____

_____

_____

Suggested Reading: Maulding Green, W. and Leonard, E. (2019). *The Soft Skills of Leadership: Navigating with Confidence and Humility* (Second Edition). Rowman & Littlefield, Lanham, MD. Chapter 3.

Additional Selected Reading: Holmes, W. T. and Parker, M. A. (2017). "Communication: Empirically Testing Behavioral Integrity and Credibility as Antecedents for the Effective Implementation of Motivating Language." *International Journal of Business Communication*, *54*(1), 70–82. doi:10.1177/2329488416675450.

EXAM TIME

You have been at your institution for just over five years. It is time for your annual evaluation and you go with some trepidation. All raises are based on performance or, more accurately, perceptions of performance. Your office has made vast strides in service and processes that improve customer service. You are very proud of these accomplishments. Unfortunately, within the last month, you discovered that your second and third in command made a decision to adjust a calendar event, final exams, without letting you know and worse, without realizing that the faculty needed to be informed. This created a huge public relations challenge.

You use the event as a teachable moment for your staff. However, you take full responsibility when notifying the university community. You are hoping that an error by your second in command will not be the focus at your annual evaluation. Now it appears likely that the calendar event error may cost you your job and put the one who made it into your position. You are not removed from the job; however, the position status is downgraded so that you no longer report directly to the chancellor. However, you will maintain your salary.

What do you do?

_____

_____

_____

_____

_____

_____

_____

Suggested Reading: Maulding Green, W., and Leonard, E. (2019). *The Soft Skills of Leadership: Navigating with Confidence and Humility* (Second Edition). Rowman & Littlefield, Lanham, MD. Chapter 3.

Additional Selected Reading: Davis, T. (2017). "Building Relationships That Work." *Chief Learning Officer, 16*(10), 20–60.

DECISIONS, DECISIONS

You have recently been hired as the university registrar at a major state institution and you are thrilled about the opportunity. The new job requires you to relocate. Your only acceptance condition is being allowed to miss one commencement ceremony. The commencement you are asking to miss will be the following year when your daughter will be graduating from college as the valedictorian of her class in another state. You are assured that this will not be a problem, so you excitedly accept the position and get to work.

When the time rolls around, you are confident all of the preplanning will allow you to attend your daughter's graduation without a hitch. You then remind your boss that you will not be at the ceremony but will be available by phone if needed. Your boss (an upper-level administrator and the person who agreed to the condition) rescinds permission just two weeks before the ceremony. She requires you to attend the work-related graduation ceremony or lose your job. You assure her that you have all contingencies accounted for and remind her that this was part of your hiring agreement. Her response is that she is glad she does not have to decide to attend her child's graduation or lose her job and reminds you, however, that you do.

What do you do?

_____

_____

_____

_____

_____

_____

_____

Suggested Reading: Maulding Green, W. and Leonard, E. (2019). *The Soft Skills of Leadership: Navigating with Confidence and Humility* (Second Edition). Rowman & Littlefield, Lanham, MD. Chapter 3.

Additional Selected Reading: Barnett, S. (2017). "ANATOMY of a LEADER: Leadership Is about Influence Rather than Authority or Titles." *Georgia Trend*, SB19.

THE END JUSTIFIES THE MEANS

You have been a full-time faculty member at your institution for several years and have recently earned the rank of associate professor. Having conducted research and subsequently presenting and publishing the findings, you understand the importance and value of research in your discipline and as a means of furthering your career.

As is the case at most institutions of higher learning, being promoted in rank at your academic department depends on having published and presented research in your academic discipline. Faculty in your department and in other disciplines across campus all work hard, but sometimes struggle to get their research published before annual evaluations so they can be considered for promotion in rank.

In all research, of course, the protection of human subjects must be considered, which means research done in your discipline requires appropriate permissions be sought and obtained, including your university's Institutional Review Board (IRB). In your fellow-faculty members' haste to complete and submit their research for conference presentations and journal publications in order to meet evaluation and promotion requirements, you become aware that some are not securing the appropriate human subjects protection permissions through the IRB. These faculty have shared that they believe having to get IRB approval is a waste of time and an unnecessary obstacle.

Securing the appropriate approvals for research involving human subjects is very important. IRBs operate under the guidelines and regulations set forth from the Department of Health and Human Services. These review boards are necessary to review research protocols to ensure research involving human subjects is carried out in an ethical and responsible manner. Furthermore, grant applications have to go through IRB approval if the research involves human subjects. Failure to comply can result in harm to the institution's status to receive federal funding from federal grant sources in the event your institution is audited and found noncompliant in this area.

You are aware that some of the faculty in your academic department are blatantly disregarding securing IRB approval when they are conducting research with human subjects (although you lack concrete proof). What do you do?

_____

_____

_____

_____

_____

_____

_____

Suggested Reading: Maulding Green, W. and Leonard, E. (2019). *The Soft Skills of Leadership: Navigating with Confidence and Humility* (Second Edition). Rowman & Littlefield, Lanham, MD. Chapter 3.

Additional Selected Reading: Beam, A. P., Claxton, R. L., and Smith, S. J. (2016). "Challenges for Novice School Leaders: Facing Today's Issues in School Administration." *Educational Leadership and Administration: Teaching and Program Development*, 27, 145–161.

POINT OF VIEW

A serious disciplinary infraction has occurred warranting dismissal from the university for four students. As Director of Student Life, you have followed procedure and recommended the students for dismissal. Your supervisor supports the action as do the provost and president. The students are dismissed from the university.

Within a week of the students' dismissal, you are summoned to the president's office for a meeting. A second individual is there who turns out to be a former board member, an active supporter of the university, and the parent of one of the resident assistants (RAs). After introductions the president says he would like you to hear what the gentleman has to say. You, of course, agree.

The parent tells you that his son was approached by two of the dismissed students and threatened with physical harm (the threat was not carried out) because they said he had "ratted them out." It was true that the man's son had provided part of the information that eventually led to the dismissal of the four students. Further, the parent says that the two dismissed students said the Director of Student Life (you) told them that his son had provided information. You share with him that you have no recollection of telling the dismissed students anything about where the information came from. The parent essentially calls you a liar and demands that you apologize to him and his son and that he will hold you personally liable should anything happen to his son because of this incident. This outburst happened quickly before you or the president could say a word.

How do you respond?

_____

_____

_____

_____

_____

_____

_____

Suggested Reading: Maulding Green, W. and Leonard, E. (2019). *The Soft Skills of Leadership: Navigating with Confidence and Humility* (Second Edition). Rowman & Littlefield, Lanham, MD. Chapter 3.

Additional Selected Reading: Molinsky, A. and Newfield, J. (2017). "How to Gain Credibility When You Have Little Experience." *Harvard Business School Cases*, 1.

CHAPTER 1

CANDID CAMERA

One of the truisms in life is that anything that can happen probably will. Even the most sensible and well thought of students can be found to have acted poorly. Such was the case when the Housing Director came to you as Director of Student Life with a videotape.

"You just have to watch this," she said.
"Why," you responded.
"Well, we have them on tape."
"What are you talking about?" you finally ask.
"One of the resident assistants saw some boys acting suspiciously and videotaped them," she explains.
"OK, what were they doing?" you ask, feeling frustrated at her drawing out the explanation.
"Standing outside the building smoking," she said.
"This is not a smoke-free campus, yet," you tell her.
"You don't understand—they were smoking pot," she outs with, at last.
"How to you know?" you ask.
"They were standing in a circle and passing the blunt from left to right."

The description is all foreign language to you. You do not know what "blunt" is and/ or what the significance of passing the alleged blunt to the right is either.

You take the tape and view it. Sure enough, there are five young men standing in circle smoking one cigarette and passing it around as described.

What do you do?

_____
_____
_____
_____
_____
_____
_____
_____

Suggested Reading: Maulding Green, W. and Leonard, E. (2019). *The Soft Skills of Leadership: Navigating with Confidence and Humility* (Second Edition). Rowman & Littlefield, Lanham, MD. Chapter 3.

Additional Selected Reading: Williams Jr., R., Raffo, D. M., and Clark, L. A. (2018). "Charisma as an Attribute of Transformational Leaders: What about Credibility?" *Journal of Management Development*, 37(6), 512–524. doi:10.1108/JMD-03-2018-0088.

2

AUTHORS' OPTIONS FOR CREDIBILITY SJTS

CLINICAL TRIALS AND TRIBULATIONS

A. Tell the faculty members (instructor and chair) that you support their decision. Too much coursework was missed and a dismissal is appropriate.

B. Tell the faculty members (instructor and chair) that the university policy requires that they allow the student to make up the missed coursework and that you will ensure that they abide by this policy.

C. Call the student in to confirm that the department chair and instructor have determined that dismissal is appropriate. Inform the student that they can submit a grade grievance at the end of the term once final grades are entered.

D. Ask the instructor and chair if the student were male, would they allow him to make up the material?

E. Other option:

_____

_____

_____

EXAM TIME

A. Your position was demoted based on the calendar event and you accept the decision without comment. After all you still have a job.

B. You bring up the unfortunate final exam error immediately to fully explain that you have your employees under control. You point out the great strides made in most areas.

C. You threaten to go to human resources (HR); this is just not fair.

D. You update your resume; it is time to find a new place to work before you are fired.

E. Other option:

_____

_____

_____

DECISIONS, DECISIONS

A. Go to HR; this is not fair.

B. Figure out if you can afford to quit your job and still pay your mortgage until you find another job.

C. Suck it up, you are an employee and serve at the pleasure of the administration.

D. Update your resume, this is a toxic environment. Best to move on.

E. Other option:

_____

_____

_____

THE END JUSTIFIES THE MEANS

A. Go talk to the IRB administrator/chair at your institution and make him or her aware of the situation.

B. Go talk to the dean and ask him or her to address the situation.

C. Email the Department of Health and Human Services to make them aware of the situation.

D. Do nothing and hope things will improve.

E. Other option:

_____

_____

_____

POINT OF VIEW

A. Tell the father that you did not implicate his son. Furthermore, he should do as he deems best from a legal point of view.

B. Tell the father that you appreciate his concern and hope that the threat is the end of the situation but that you did not implicate his son. Furthermore, he should do as he deems best from a legal point of view.

C. Allow the president to respond to the parent. He obviously has known him for some time and can better answer the parent.

D. Apologize profusely to the parent asked. But, tell the parent that you will have your attorney deal with any liability issues.

E. Other option:

_____

_____

_____

CANDID CAMERA

A. Show your supervisor the tape and seek her advice.

B. Call in the RAs who taped the students and get their input.

C. Do some research to make sure you know the verbiage; then call in the students one by one keeping them separated and confront each one.

D. Write the incident off as a bad situation that is irresolvable.

E. Other option:

_____

_____

_____

3

LESSONS ON COMPETENCE

Professional competence requires constant renewal. Higher education leaders, whether at public or private or proprietary junior/community colleges or four-year colleges or universities, come from a variety of backgrounds. Some rise through the ranks in higher education, while others join the ranks of higher education leaders (e.g., especially upper-echelon leaders such as presidents, provosts, or specialists in accounting or athletics) from areas outside higher education. Regardless of the path to leadership, these individuals must master their trade and doing so requires constant renewal and an unwavering devotion to lifelong learning. The credo of higher education leaders, like that of leaders in all areas, should be that they will remain current and thoroughly knowledgeable in their field. That they will be competent in their chosen field.

The scenarios in this chapter are, in one way or another, related to a leader's Competence. If your Leader Acumen assessment scores indicate this as an area for needed growth, you should work through the scenarios with a couple of things in mind. First, as you work through the scenarios in the chapter, take particular note of the *Authors' Options* to each problem at the end of each chapter of SJTs. In working through the scenarios and reviewing the *Authors' Options*, one of two things will happen. You will find disparity between your responses and the authors, or you might, indeed, find that your responses coincide with the authors' (see Appendix B, for a graphic representation). Next, reflect on the information you gained from the LSI assessment. If you acknowledge that Competence is an area for growth based on the assessment, ask yourself if this was based on your Self-assessment, the Circle assessment, or both.

If either or both assessments (the Self or Circle) indicate that you have room for improvement in the area of leader Competence *and* you are also finding disparity in yours and the *Authors' Options*, chances are that you will find growth via working through these exercises and accompanying readings. However, be reminded, this will not happen overnight. Growing your *Leader Acumen* is a worthy endeavor but is a painstakingly time-consuming undertaking. It requires rewiring of your thought processes regarding learnings that are very much ingrained into your most innate thought processes and this takes time (see Appendix B for a graphic representation).

On the other hand, if you find your solutions and the solutions offered in the *Authors' Options* coincide highly, yet your Self score is lower than the mean shown at the end of your LSI assessment for Competence, one of two things is happening. Either you are lacking in self-confidence, yet your decision-making is solid, or perhaps you are somewhat overconfident but nonetheless making good decisions. If the first is the case, working through the scenarios should enhance your self-confidence. The second option (overconfidence) is the one to be most wary of. Leaders in this category many times find themselves derailed as leaders, even though they generally are good decision makers. Working through the scenarios should help in instilling the idea that there is more than one acceptable solution to most problem/issues and thus lessen one potential major consequence of overconfidence, feeling that you have the only viable solution.

If you opt to have a Circle/360-assessment done and find that your solutions and the solutions offered in the *Authors' Options* coincide highly, yet your Circle scores are outside the standard deviation (available from the LEAD team when a Circle/360-assessment is done) LEA for Competence, it is possible that a different set of problems is occurring. Either you are selecting the course of action you believe is best for the scenario, yet in reality you would not implement it, or the problem may be one of *perception*. It is much more likely that it is the former. Only in rare instances would the latter be the case. However, we insert it here for thought because, on occasion, it is the case. And, as the old saying goes, perception is reality.

Perhaps you are indeed highly competent yet *perception* is the issue for your low scores in Competence. This could be a case of projection. For example, you may not "look" competent and perhaps for legitimate reasons. You will recall from the chapter on credibility in volume 1 that mention was made of how "what you wear" infers or projects an image. Such could be the case in this instance.

Finally, improving your Leader Acumen and "adaptive capacity," as stated in the preface, is a process. As you will recall, the notion of Leader Acumen is predicated on the theory that there is a genetic predisposition toward leadership.

As Marquis and Tilscik[1] so aptly noted, imprinting may take place, during brief sensitive periods of high susceptibility during the formative process, during the teachable moment or another yet different time of susceptibility, and that imprints once established are persistent.

The lessons in this book are to be utilized to grow LSI in this third way—over the long, repetitive process. To that end and to truly be imprinted with any of the competencies, actions for building the various skillsets may be found in Appendix C.

Again, quoting volume 1, "true competence in effectively applying 'hard skills' requires mastery of 'soft skills'—that is, people-centered skills."[2]

PRACTICE WHAT YOU PREACH

You oversee academic advising for undergraduate students in your college. The advising office employs three academic advisors and one academic records specialist. The advisors are responsible for ensuring that students are supported in their progress toward degree, that they are enrolled in appropriate coursework, and that they learn about supplemental services on campus. The advisors specialize in knowing all degree requirements for the majors in your college. The academic records specialist is a clerical support position that serves students and advisors but has no authority to advice students regarding required coursework.

In preparation for new student orientation, the advisors review students' records the day before orientation and have the option to preregister students for a freshman year experience (FYE) course. They then prepare a list of coursework that the student needs to register for during orientation. Students in your college are able to opt out of the FYE course if they would like to do so during orientation. During orientation, the advisors meet with each student to describe the required coursework. The academic records specialist supports the process of registration for the students. She is aware of her boundaries and knows her role is support and not to advise students regarding coursework. She is a good person who cares a great deal about students.

You attend orientation at the student center to support the advisors and academic records specialist. All students of your college **were** in one room. Students from the other colleges at the university are organized into different rooms by college. Your group finishes early and is able to return to the office, while others are still advising. After returning to the office, the academic records specialist approaches you to talk. Her concern is about how an advisor from another college mistreated her. She states that after your group was finished with registration, she went into the room of a different college to see a family friend (an incoming freshman majoring in a different college). She reveals that the family friend was frustrated she had not yet met with her advisor and that she had been waiting for twenty-five minutes. The academic records specialist had informed the advisor that the student had been waiting for a long period of time and needed advising. The advisor told her, "I'll be with her shortly, as soon as I've finished with the student I'm working with." You sense there is more to the story when she says "I just wanted you to know if you get a call from the advisor."

The following day you receive a formal complaint from the advisor who had worked with the family friend. The advisor stated that the academic records specialist rudely told her that she needed to see her family friend who had been waiting too long. She said that the academic records specialist then went back to talk with the family friend and eventually left the room, only to return a little while later to talk again with the family friend, and then left again. The advisor then stated that the academic records specialist had left the room to request that the registrar's office remove the student from a FYE course. The registrar's office was familiar with the academic records specialist and therefore removed the student from the course believing this was a student in your college.

Once the advisor was able to meet with the family friend, she saw that the student had been removed from the FYE course. In investigating how the student had been removed from the course, she learned that the academic records specialist had made the request. The FYE course was required for this student's major. She had been pre registered for the course to ensure that she had a seat in the course. Now the course was full and the advisor had to appeal to the instructor to allow the student back into the course.

After reading the formal complaint, you sit down with the academic records specialist to ask if she had taken action to remove her family friend from a freshman year experience course. She said, "Well, somebody had to help her since the advisor wouldn't. My family friend wanted out of the course and I was able to help. Don't you want me to help students at this institution?"

What will you do?

_____

_____

_____

_____

_____

_____

_____

Suggested Reading: Maulding Green, W. and Leonard, E. (2019). *The Soft Skills of Leadership: Navigating with Confidence and Humility.* (Second Edition). Rowman & Littlefield, Lanham, MD. Chapter 4.

Additional Selected Reading: Giles, Sunnie. (2016). "The Most Important Leadership Competencies, According to Leaders around the World." Retrieved from https://hbr.org/2016/03/the-most-important-leadership-competencies-according-to-leaders-around-the-world.

THE GOOD, THE BAD, AND THE UGLY

You are a well-respected faculty member in the academic department of your institution. The majority of the faculty and staff in your academic department are hardworking and put forth great effort in their daily tasks of educating students. Despite these hardworking efforts by the faculty and staff, morale in your academic department is low. Faculty are constantly having conversations among themselves about the state of affairs within the academic department. The complaints and concerns of faculty are common within the realm of academia and higher education—specifically, there are issues regarding academic rigor, salary, rude student behavior, and lack of support from administration. While faculty understand that salaries might not be what they want, they are becoming increasingly frustrated with students being able to complain to the dean and "get their way" in many areas, such as enrolling in classes late, misrepresenting what faculty say (and thereby the dean overriding what faculty say), and missing important programmatic deadlines.

Unfortunately, these frustrations have led to a larger percentage of faculty attrition than normal, when compared to previous years. A few of the remaining veteran faculty have spoken with the dean regarding the concerns, and the dean acts as if there is no problem or the concerns are not warranted. The dean claims to make efforts in addressing these concerns as much as possible, although this is not evident to all.

Some faculty have encouraged the dean to send out a questionnaire to faculty and staff to see what current concerns exist in the academic department. The dean refuses to do this, and some of the faculty are becoming more frustrated because of this lack of action. Since assuming the deanship, many at the institution believe that the dean has plans of career advancement at the institution. Therefore, it appears the concerns will not be addressed in hopes no one from outside the academic department notices. As a veteran faculty member, you share the same concerns and frustrations as other faculty members and staff.

What do you do?

_____

_____

_____

_____

_____

_____

_____

Suggested Reading: Maulding Green, W. and Leonard, E. (2019). *The Soft Skills of Leadership: Navigating with Confidence and Humility* (Second Edition). Rowman & Littlefield, Lanham, MD. Chapter 4.

Additional Selected Reading: Gukdo, B., Ye, D., Soojin, L., and Seungwan, K. (2017). "Leader Trust, Competence, LMX, and Member Performance: A Moderated Mediation Framework." *Psychological Reports*, *120*(6), 1137–1159. doi:10.1177/0033294117716465.

THE EMBATTLED DEAN

You are provost at a mid-sized university. The longest-serving college dean has been a friend and colleague for more than twenty years. The college is in the preliminary stages of its five-year reaccreditation process. Recently, the university announced that the college would be named for a prominent local family that has donated several million dollars to create an endowment to support capital improvements, scholarships, and faculty recognition programs.

You are surprised to learn that a majority of the tenured faculty members of the college have met in private and voted a resolution of "no confidence" in the dean's continued leadership. The resolution urges the university administration to remove the dean from his position, citing poor communication skills, an autocratic management style that minimizes faculty participation in key decisions, and lack of an inclusive strategic planning processes. The resolution further states that these deficiencies jeopardize the college's reaccreditation. One of the disgruntled faculty members has sent a copy of the resolution to the donor and to the local newspaper, which has published an article about the situation.

What should you do?

_____

_____

_____

_____

_____

_____

_____

Suggested Reading: Maulding Green, W. and Leonard, E. (2019). *The Soft Skills of Leadership: Navigating with Confidence and Humility* (Second Edition). Rowman & Littlefield, Lanham, MD. Chapter 4.

Additional Selected Reading: Portnova, I. and Peiseniece, L. (2017). "Leaders' Competences for Successful Leadership of Invention and Implementation of Innovation: A Conceptual Model." *Journal of Business Management, 2017*(13), 40–55.

WHAT DID YOU SAY?

It is very near the end of the current term when an incident occurred in a senior class in the English department. A student (in the presence of the entire class) expressed her opinion of the teacher and the teacher's teaching and grading practices with an expletive-filled rant lasting two or three minutes. The student then stormed out the classroom leaving everyone, teacher and students, dumbfounded. The report of the incident is on your desk the next day.

Per policy and procedure, you start arranging for a disciplinary hearing for the student. The student is a commuter and it takes several attempts before you are finally able to contact her and tell her of the planned meeting. Three faculty members compose the committee that is charged with determining the punishment, if any, to be meted out to the student. As you are briefing the committee on the incident prior to calling the student in (she is waiting outside the hearing room), the provost enters the room. Without prelude, he declares that the student is to be notified that she is dismissed from the university.

What do you do?

_____

_____

_____

_____

_____

_____

_____

Suggested Reading: Maulding Green, W. and Leonard, E. (2019). *The Soft Skills of Leadership: Navigating with Confidence and Humility* (Second Edition). Rowman & Littlefield, Lanham, MD. Chapter 4.

Additional Selected Reading: Minh, N. V., Badir, Y. F., Quang, N. N., and Afsar, B. (2017). "The Impact of Leaders' Technical Competence on Employees' Innovation and Learning." *Journal of Engineering and Technology Management*, 44, 44–57. doi:10.1016/j.jengtecman.2017.03.003.

CHOICES, CHOICES

You are a young first-year, first-time head coach and are charged with hiring your coaching staff. You have hired assistant coaches you know well and who are your contemporaries. You all have equal experience and knowledgeable about your sport. For your final hire, you have two candidates. The first is another qualified young candidate who is also your friend. You are confident this person will be energetic and loyal. The second is an older, former head coach who has more experience and knowledge than you.

What do you do?

_____

_____

_____

_____

_____

_____

_____

Suggested Reading: Maulding Green, W. and Leonard, E. (2019). *The Soft Skills of Leadership: Navigating with Confidence and Humility* (Second Edition). Rowman & Littlefield, Lanham, MD. Chapter 4.

Additional Selected Reading: Postuła, A. and Majczyk, J. (2018). "Managers and Leaders in Need of Entrepreneurial Competences." *Entrepreneurial Business and Economics Review*, 6(1), 91–103. doi:10.15678/EBER.2018.060105.

AND THE FINAL SCORE IS?

As vice president, you see the annual reviews of the secretaries and administrative assistants in your area. On a five-point scale, everyone is getting a five, which makes the evaluation meaningless.

What do you do?

_____

_____

_____

_____

_____

_____

_____

Suggested Reading: Maulding Green, W. and Leonard, E. (2019). *The Soft Skills of Leadership: Navigating with Confidence and Humility* (Second Edition). Rowman & Littlefield, Lanham, MD. Chapter 4.

Additional Selected Reading: Wang, N., Wilhite, S., and Martino, D. (2016). "Understanding the Relationship between School Leaders' Social and Emotional Competence and Their Transformational Leadership: The Importance of Self-Other Agreement." *Educational Management Administration & Leadership*, 44(3), 467–490.

BLOWING IN THE WIND

Each morning, when you arrive at work, on your desk is the campus security report for the previous evening and night. All of the items are routine with little need for follow-up. For example, ten of the twelve items on the list are notes that a student returned to campus after midnight, the normal closing time for the dorms. However, one item catches your attention, a female student was identified as having and using the ooga horn on her car to get the attention of students walking around campus.

According to the report, she sounded the horn at least twenty times during the evening and early night before entering her dorm for the night. Added to this notation was a brief note from the food service director that she had come into the cafeteria inappropriately dressed. She had on a see-through blouse and no upper body undergarments. These are not the first two complaints about this student; she has a significant record of questionable behavior and is known to be argumentative. She is on probationary status for the prior problems and has been told that further problems will result in her dismissal from the university. She is on scholarship as an out-of-state student and has connections to members of the upper-level university administration.

What do you do?

_____

_____

_____

_____

_____

_____

_____

_____

Suggested Reading: Maulding Green, W. and Leonard, E. (2019). *The Soft Skills of Leadership: Navigating with Confidence and Humility* (Second Edition). Rowman & Littlefield, Lanham, MD. Chapter 4.

Additional Selected Reading: Gupta, M., and Bhal, K. T. (2017). "LMX & Leader Competence: Impact on Subordinates' Perceived Cohesion." *Indian Journal of Industrial Relations*, *53*(2), 277–289.

AUTHORS' OPTIONS FOR COMPETENCE SJTS

PRACTICE WHAT YOU PREACH

A. Tell the academic records specialist that you want her to help all students at the university.

B. Tell the academic records specialist that while you want her to support students, this is not something she is allowed to do because the student was from a different college. Ask that she apologize to the advisor and never do this again.

C. Call the student to hear her side of the story.

D. Defend the actions of your academic records specialist to the complaining advisor.

E. Other option:

_____

_____

_____

THE GOOD, THE BAD, AND THE UGLY

A. Talk to the dean again and once more suggest a morale check of the faculty and staff.

B. Schedule an appointment with the provost and tell him or her about the situation. Request action be taken before there is a mass exodus of faculty.

C. Take no action but continue doing the best job as possible given the circumstances.

D. Begin talking to other deans at the institution to see if they have ideas as how the situation might be handled.

E. Other option:

_____

_____

_____

THE EMBATTLED DEAN

A. Reject the "no confidence" vote and issue a statement in support of the dean.
B. Tell the faculty leaders that the resolution should be withdrawn because it has led to negative publicity that adversely affects the positive news about the endowment and threatens to put at risk further support from donors.
C. Meet with the entire faculty of the college, listening to both critics and supporters of the dean and offering confidential meetings for faculty members who are reluctant to speak publicly.
D. Conduct a 360-degree performance review of the dean.
E. Other option:

_____

_____

_____

WHAT DID YOU SAY?

A. Follow the provost's direction and dismiss the student.
B. Tell the provost that his action violates policy and due process and cannot be allowed.
C. Tell the provost that you will appeal his unilateral decision to the president.
D. Dismiss the committee and ask the provost to stay and speak to you privately. Express your concerns about potential policy and due process violations and tell him that he will have to put in writing his directive to dismiss the student.
E. Other option:

_____

_____

_____

CHOICES, CHOICES

A. Thoroughly research the background of the former head coach to be comfortable that he will not undermine you, and hire the experienced coach.

B. Hiring one more friend completes the circle of loyalty. Hire the friend and all of you learn together.
C. Seek other applicants for the position with comparable backgrounds to ensure a good selection.
D. Postpone a decision and go with one less coach.
E. Other option:

_____

_____

_____

AND THE FINAL SCORE IS?

A. Redline the reviews and require staff responsible for the reviews to do them again.
B. Meet with staff who are responsible for the reviews and discuss making the reviews more meaningful.
C. Meet with staff who are responsible for the reviews and tell them that in your opinion none of the personnel they reviewed deserve all fives.
D. Meet individually with each staff member who is responsible for the reviews and ask them for an explanation of why the reviews were all fives.
E. Other option:

_____

_____

_____

BLOWING IN THE WIND

A. Call her connections and get them to intercede hoping they can have a positive influence.
B. Act according to the prescribed procedure for a student on probation.
C. Meet with your supervisor, explain the situation, and let her decide what to do.
D. Call her in and reprimand and caution her about causing further problems.
E. Other option:

_____

_____

_____

❺

LESSONS ON ABILITY
TO INSPIRE

When our intent as a leader is to inspire, we often fall short of our goal. For some reason, as leaders, we believe that inspiration is some mystical/magical force that only coaches and motivational speakers possess. Although inspiration can sometimes take the form of inclusion of the elements of high energy and mountain-moving motivation, inspiration is best achieved through what we do and say.

The scenarios in this chapter are, in one way or another, related to a leader's ABILITY to INSPIRE. If your Leader Acumen assessment scores indicate this as an area for needed growth, you should work through the scenarios with a couple of things in mind. First, as you work through the scenarios in the chapter, take particular note of the *Authors' Options* to each problem at the end of each chapter of SJTs. In working through the scenarios and reviewing the *Authors' Options*, one of two things will happen. You will find disparity between your responses and the authors, or you might, indeed, find that your responses coincide with the authors' (see Appendix B for a graphic representation). Next, reflect on the information you gained from the LEA assessment. If you acknowledge that Ability to Inspire is an area for growth based on the assessment, ask yourself if this was based on your Self-assessment, the Circle assessment, or both.

If either or both assessments (the Self or Circle) indicate that you have room for improvement in the area of leader Ability to Inspire *and* you are also finding disparity in yours and the *Authors' Options*, chances are you will find growth via working through these exercises and accompanying readings. However, be reminded, this will not happen overnight. Growing your *Leader Acumen* is a worthy endeavor but is a painstakingly time-consuming undertaking. It requires rewiring of your thought processes regarding learnings that are very much ingrained into your most innate thought processes and this takes time (see Appendix B for a graphic representation).

On the other hand, if you find your solutions and the solutions offered in the *Authors' Options* coincide highly, yet your Self score is lower than the mean shown at the end of your LSI assessment for Ability to Inspire, one of two things is happening. Either you are lacking in self-confidence, yet your decision-making is solid, or perhaps you are somewhat overconfident but nonetheless making good decisions. If the first is the case, working through the scenarios should enhance your self-confidence. The second option (overconfidence) is the one to be most wary of. Leaders in this category many times find themselves derailed as leaders, even though they generally are good decision makers. Working through the scenarios should help in instilling the idea that there is more than one acceptable solution to most problem/issues and thus lessen one potential major consequence of overconfidence, feeling that you have the only viable solution.

If you opt to have a Circle/360-assessment done and find that your solutions and the solutions offered in the *Authors' Options* coincide highly, yet your Circle scores were outside the standard deviation (available from the LEAD team when a Circle/360-assessment is done) LEA for Ability to Inspire, it is possible that a different set of problems is occurring. Either you are selecting the course of action you believe is best for the scenario, yet in reality you would not implement it, or the problem may be one of *perception*. It is much more likely that it is the former. Only in rare instances would the latter be the case. However, we insert it here for thought because, on occasion, it is the case. And, as the old saying goes, perception is reality.

Perhaps you are indeed highly inspirational yet *perception* is the issue for your low scores in Ability to Inspire. This could be a case of projection. For example, you may not appear inspirational and perhaps for legitimate reasons. You will recall from the chapter on credibility in Volume 1 that mention was made of how "what you wear" infers or projects an image. Such could be the case in this instance.

Finally, improving your Leader Acumen and "adaptive capacity," as stated in the preface, is a process. As you will recall, the notion of Leader Acumen is predicated on the theory that there is a genetic predisposition toward leadership.

As Marquis and Tilscik[1] so aptly noted, imprinting may take place, during brief sensitive periods of high susceptibility during the formative process, during the teachable moment or another yet different time of susceptibility, and that imprints once established are persistent.

The lessons in this book are to be utilized to grow Leader Acumen in this third way—over the long, repetitive process. To that end and to truly be imprinted with any of the competencies, actions for building the various skillsets may be found in Appendix C.

"True inspiration for both the leader and peers and followers comes from within by finding value and meaning in the work they do."

FACT OR FICTION?

As a faculty member at your institution with past experience in accreditation, you have become aware of some information that is very concerning. Another faculty member who has been assigned to handle all of your academic department's accreditation efforts has said and done some things that are questionable at best and devastating at worst.

One day, while you were having an informal meeting with the department chair, the faculty member responsible for your department's accreditation efforts comes into the department chair's office and, during the conversation, says that he is changing data that will go into an accreditation report. You speak up and tell him that he should not do that, but then he brushes your comment aside and leaves shortly thereafter. After he leaves, you ask the department chair his thoughts about the situation, and he acts as though the conversation never occurred.

This faculty member has been responsible for the department's accreditation efforts and reports for several years. Faculty members in the department joke that the department's accreditation reports are works of "fiction" and this faculty member should be a best-selling author. He once composed a report that drew national accolades in areas that were not even close the academic offerings of your academic department. When this happened, some faculty members complained to the dean, but the dean did nothing. You have spoken with the dean about the situation, including the incident that happened in the meeting with the chair. The dean has assured you she will address the problem, but nothing has happened and that was several months ago. The faculty member continues writing accreditation reports for the academic department.

What should you do?

_____

_____

_____

_____

_____

_____

_____

Suggested Reading: Maulding Green, W. and Leonard, E. (2019). *The Soft Skills of Leadership: Navigating with Confidence and Humility* (Second Edition). Rowman & Littlefield, Lanham, MD. Chapter 5.

Additional Selected Reading: Hoffner, L. A. (2018). "Leadership Is More Than a Noun." *Parks & Recreation*, 53(5), 50.

FOOTBALL FRENZY

After a nationwide search, you have been appointed president of a doctoral-level regional university. For athletic competition, the university is classified Division I but is the only school in the twelve-member conference that does not field an intercollegiate football team. In fact, the university is the only public four-year public institution in the state that does not have a football program. The conference has announced that, within five years, only schools that play football will be allowed to remain in the conference.

During interviews, you are questioned about your attitude toward starting a football program. You gather that there is great enthusiasm for football among undergraduate students and alumni, skepticism from faculty leaders, and mixed feelings among board members. You manage to avoid being pinned down on the issue, claiming you need time to conduct a thorough feasibility assessment.

In the first month on the job, you are approached by two influential board members, both alumni and major donors, who urge you to bring a resolution to the next board meeting recommending that the university immediately begin the process of starting a Division I football program. Your preliminary review of the university's financial condition has made you very uncomfortable with the notion of undertaking such a costly initiative at this time.

What should you do?

_____

_____

_____

_____

_____

_____

_____

Suggested Reading: Maulding Green, W. and Leonard, E. (2019). *The Soft Skills of Leadership: Navigating with Confidence and Humility* (Second Edition). Rowman & Littlefield, Lanham, MD. Chapter 5.

Additional Selected Reading: Fransen, K., Vande Broek, G., Boen, F., Steffens, N. K., Haslam, S. A., and Vanbeselaere, N. (2016). "We Will Be Champions: Leaders' Confidence in 'Us' Inspires Team Members' Team Confidence and Performance." *Scandinavian Journal of Medicine & Science in Sports*, 26(12), 1455–1469.

TIME IS NOT LIMITLESS

The normal work day for staff at the institution is eight hours with an hour for lunch. Everyone is expected to arrive at 8:00 a.m. and depart not earlier that 5:00 p.m. And then, there are the directors under your supervision as Director of Student Life: the Housing Director and the Director of Student Activities. The latter of the positions especially calls for a great deal of evening and night responsibility (after the normal working day) though the Housing Director is often called on for after-normal hours work as you are. Newly appointed as Director of Student Life, they come to you seeking redress for what they feel is wrong with having to put in extra hours for no extra pay and no comp time. You know extra pay is out of the question as the university budget is tighter than ever. Comp time seems like a viable solution. But the directors are asking for hour-for-hour comp time.

You have looked up the regulations (that apply to private sector employers, and you work for a private university) and find that "the Fair Labor Standards Act (FLSA) allows both public *and private* sector employers to offer comp time to their *exempt* employees." You also discover that "unlike comp time for public sector non-exempt employees, 'comp time' for exempt employees can be granted in any form the employer chooses." You could elect to give exempt employees one hour of "comp time" for every hour over forty. You could grant "comp time" after 50 hours, after 160 hours in a month, or in any other manner you choose. The university has no comp time policy.

What should you do?

_____

_____

_____

_____

_____

_____

_____

Suggested Reading: Maulding Green, W. and Leonard, E. (2019). *The Soft Skills of Leadership: Navigating with Confidence and Humility* (Second Edition). Rowman & Littlefield, Lanham, MD. Chapter 5.

Additional Selected Reading: Bawany, S. (2016). "Leadership during Turbulent Times." *Leadership Excellence Essentials*, *33*(12), 18.

Quotation from: Wage and Hour Insights. (2015). "Can Employers Offer Compensatory Time to Exempt Employees?" Retrieved from https://www.wagehourinsights.com/2015/07/can-employers-offer-compensatory-time-to-exempt-employees-wage-hour-faq/.

THE TRUTH AND NOTHING BUT THE TRUTH

An excellent faculty member has applied for tenure. He is recommended at both the department and college levels and now you, as the vice president, have recommended tenure. The president turns it down. The rationale offered by the president is that the faculty member was presumed to have had consensual sex with an adult student. You have good reason to believe that the president's reasons are personal and the rationale is a ruse.

The faculty member files a grievance. Your handbook does not allow you to tell him the recommendation at any level of administration.

What do you do?

_____

_____

_____

_____

_____

_____

_____

_____

Suggested Reading: Maulding Green, W. and Leonard, E. (2019). *The Soft Skills of Leadership: Navigating with Confidence and Humility* (Second Edition). Rowman & Littlefield, Lanham, MD. Chapter 5.

Additional Selected Reading: Heller, J., Notgrass, D., and Conner, C. (2017). "Moderators to the Relationship between Leaders' Inspirational Behaviors and Followers' Extra Effort." *International Journal of Business and Public Administration (IJBPA)*, 14(1), 36.

A VOICE IN THE WILDERNESS

As dean, you call a meeting to propose the first doctoral degree at your university. You invite everyone you can think of who might be involved in the decision-making process. After the meeting, several long-time members of the faculty speak out against the proposal. They believe the resources will not be available and it is a waste of time and effort to try.

What do you do?

_____
_____
_____
_____
_____
_____
_____

Suggested Reading: Maulding Green, W. and Leonard, E. (2019). *The Soft Skills of Leadership: Navigating with Confidence and Humility* (Second Edition). Rowman & Littlefield, Lanham, MD. Chapter 5.

Additional Selected Reading: Beck, M. (2016). "From Leader to an Inspiring Leader." *Leadership Excellence Essentials*, *33*(2), 40.

THE ROAD LESS TRAVELED

You arrive as a new administrator on a young campus. The school does not have the tradition or resources at this time to be a research university but aspires for this status in the future. Currently, all of the faculty are reviewed against the same teaching, research, and service criteria. However, the talents of the faculty are varied across the fields of teaching and research. You have come from a research institution that allowed evaluation with variable criteria where faculty with excellent research abilities were given a reduced teaching load but with increased expectations for scholarship. People with stronger teaching interests were given a heavier teaching load with a reduced expectation for scholarship.

What do you do?

_____

_____

_____

_____

_____

_____

_____

_____

Suggested Reading: Maulding Green, W. and Leonard, E. (2019). *The Soft Skills of Leadership: Navigating with Confidence and Humility* (Second Edition). Rowman & Littlefield, Lanham, MD. Chapter 5.

Additional Selected Reading: Garton, E. (2017). "How to Be an Inspiring Leader." *Harvard Business School Cases*, 1.

6

AUTHORS' OPTIONS FOR ABILITY TO INSPIRE SJTS

FACT OR FICTION?

A. Discuss your concerns with the institution's vice president of accreditation.
B. Bring up the topic for discussion at the next departmental faculty meeting.
C. Do nothing since the dean said she is going to address the situation.
D. Report the concerns to your institution's accrediting bodies.
E. Other options:

_____

_____

_____

FOOTBALL FRENZY

A. Tell the trustees you have more pressing priorities and will give football serious consideration in due time.
B. Put the matter on the board agenda for open discussion at the next meeting as requested by the trustees.
C. Ask the faculty senate to pass a resolution at its next meeting in support of or in opposition to football.
D. Refer the trustees to the director of athletics, inasmuch as he or she should be the person making the recommendation to start football.
E. Assure the trustees that consideration of football is a high priority for you and that when you and the administrative team have exercised due diligence to determine

if the timing is right to consider football, you will recommend to the board that a comprehensive feasibility study be undertaken.

F. Other option:

_____

_____

_____

TIME IS NOT LIMITLESS

A. Authorize the comp time on the basis they want, hour for hour.
B. Deny them comp time but agree to ask for a pay raise for each of them.
C. Discuss the situation with your supervisor and recommend that a policy be adopted.
D. Take no action citing current practice that no comp time is offered.
E. Other option:

_____

_____

_____

THE TRUTH AND NOTHING BUT THE TRUTH

A. Tell him anyway. It is only fair and will probably become known anyway.
B. Refer him to a higher authority in the chain of command.
C. Follow the published handbook and do not tell him.
D. Seek a change in the handbook.
E. Other option:

_____

_____

_____

A VOICE IN THE WILDERNESS

A. Meet with the opposing group to try to sway their opinion.
B. Find the people who are supportive and develop the new doctoral program.
C. Set the idea aside for future exploration.
D. Make the decision unilaterally to move forward.

E. Other option:

_____

_____

_____

THE ROAD LESS TRAVELED

A. Change the process unilaterally.

B. Leave the process as is.

C. Pass the problem to higher authorities.

D. Convince the Senate and administrators to change to the variable job description.

E. Other option:

_____

_____

_____

7

LESSONS ON VISION

In *The Soft Skills of Leadership: Navigating with Confidence and Humility*, the authors share that "vision as defined in the Leader Acumen model is the end result of a process whereby a leader develops objectives or goals and sets a direction for an organization based on the shared input of all stakeholders. Defining vision is simple. Creating a shared vision and, more significantly, effectively communicating that shared vision, and transforming it into action is the challenge."[1]

The scenarios in this chapter are, in one way or another, related to a leader's Vision. If your Leader Acumen assessment scores indicate this as an area for needed growth, you should work through the scenarios with a couple of things in mind. First, as you work through the scenarios in the chapter, take particular note of the *Authors' Options* to each problem at the end of each chapter of SJTs. In working through the scenarios and reviewing the *Authors' Options*, one of two things will happen. You will find disparity between your responses and the authors, or you might, indeed, find that your responses coincide with the authors' (see Appendix B for a graphic representation). Next, reflect on the information you gained from the LSI assessment. If you acknowledge that Vision is an area for growth based on the assessment, ask yourself if this was based on your Self-assessment, the Circle assessment, or both.

If either or both assessments (the Self or Circle) indicate that you have room for improvement in the area of leader Vision *and* you are also finding disparity in yours and the *Authors' Options*, chances are you will find growth via working through these exercises and accompanying readings. However, be reminded, this will not happen overnight. Growing your Leader Acumen is a worthy endeavor but is a painstakingly time-consuming undertaking. It requires rewiring of your thought processes regarding learnings that are very much ingrained into your most innate thought processes and this takes time (see Appendix B for a graphic representation).

On the other hand, if you find your solutions and the solutions offered in the *Authors' Options* coincide highly, yet your Self score is lower than the mean shown at the end of your LSI assessment for Vision, one of two things is happening. Either you are lacking in self-confidence, yet your decision-making is solid, or perhaps you are somewhat overconfident but nonetheless making good decisions. If the first is the case, working through the scenarios should enhance your self-confidence. The second option (overconfidence) is the one to be most wary of. Leaders in this category many times find themselves derailed as leaders, even though they generally are good decision makers. Working through the scenarios should help in instilling the idea that there is more than one acceptable solution to most problem/issues and thus lessen one potential major consequence of overconfidence, feeling that you have the only viable solution.

If you opt to have a Circle/360-assessment done and find that your solutions and the solutions offered in the *Authors' Options* coincide highly, yet your Circle scores were outside the standard deviation (available from the LEAD team when a Circle/360-assessment is done) LSI for Vision, it is possible that a different set of problems is occurring. Either you are selecting the course of action you believe is best for the scenario, yet in reality you would not implement it, or the problem may be one of *perception*. It is much more likely that it is the former. Only in rare instances would the latter be the case. However, we insert it here for thought because, on occasion, it is the case. And, as the old saying goes, perception is reality.

Perhaps you are indeed highly visionary yet perception is the issue for your low scores in Vision. This could be a case of projection. For example, you may not appear visionary and perhaps for legitimate reasons. You will recall from the chapter on credibility in Volume 1 that mention was made of how "what you wear" infers or projects an image. Such could be the case in this instance.

Finally, improving your Leader Acumen and "adaptive capacity," as stated in the preface, is a process. As you will recall, the notion of Leader Acumen is predicated on the theory that there is a genetic predisposition toward leadership.

As Marquis and Tilscik[1] so aptly noted, imprinting may take place, during brief sensitive periods of high susceptibility during the formative process, during the teachable moment or another yet different time of susceptibility, and that imprints once established are persistent.

The lessons in this book are to be utilized to grow Leader Acumen in this third way—over the long, repetitive process. To that end and to truly be imprinted with any of the competencies, actions for building the various skillsets may be found in Appendix C.

"Vision opens the door to opportunities for success for the credible, competent, inspirational leader."[2]

READY FOR A PROMOTION?

You have been a full-time faculty member at your institution for four years and recently earned the rank of associate professor. You were hired to design and coordinate a new academic program within your department. As a matter of fact, this is only the program of its nature at your institution, so this is unchartered territory for many.

Most of the faculty in your area have little to no experience and knowledge with designing, implementing, and managing programs; fortunately, you possess expertise in this area. While faculty have been supportive of your efforts, your academic dean has not. Several of the faculty perceive the dean to be a bully and try to avoid him as much as possible. It appears the dean is envious of the successful new program and has attempted to undermine your efforts. This has made managing and coordinating more stressful and difficult than necessary.

During this time, a newly created departmental chair position has been added in your academic department. This department is flourishing due to the success of the new program, and it has benefited the school and the overall institution, in general. You apply for the position and meet all of the minimal qualifications and two of the three preferred qualifications. The other applicant, an internal candidate, met the minimal qualifications and one of the preferred qualifications and has the rank of assistant professor. The other internal applicant has been working at the institution one year longer than you, but you have more years of experience in higher education. The search committee for the position consists of the dean and three handpicked faculty members.

A few days after the interviews are conducted, the dean comes to your office to hand-deliver a letter. The letter states you are not selected for the position because you did not meet the minimum qualifications. The letter is signed by the dean and the chair of the interview committee. Later you learn that the other candidate (the colleague who had been working at the institution one year longer than you) was selected for the position.

Off the record, you speak with the HR director about those minimum qualifications. The HR director (a personal friend) states you did meet the minimum qualifications as well as two of the preferred qualifications and shares that the letter you received was inaccurate. The HR director is familiar with the dean and his behavior and could offer no advice that would not cause major strife.

What do you do?

_____

_____

_____

_____

_____

_____

_____

Suggested Reading: Maulding Green, W. and Leonard, E. (2019). *The Soft Skills of Leadership: Navigating with Confidence and Humility* (Second Edition). Rowman & Littlefield, Lanham, MD. Chapter 6.

Additional Selected Reading: Smith, B. L. (2017). "A Case Study of How a Leader's Communication of Organizational Vision Influences the Development of Work Passion" (Order No. 10286682). Available from ProQuest Dissertations & Theses Global. (1925954334). Retrieved from http://lynx.lib.usm.edu/login?url=https://search-proquest-com.lynx.lib.usm.edu/docview/1925954334?accountid=13946.

HOUSTON . . . WE HAVE A PROBLEM

Your school has recently hired a new dean who is enthusiastic and very charismatic but who also aspires for the presidency. While the new dean has a terminal degree and several years of practical experience in the field, she has very little, if any, higher education administration experience.

Your school is proposing a new doctoral program that has several problems that must be addressed before the program should be submitted to gain approval for implementation. A group of faculty meet with the new dean to discuss these concerns; nonetheless, she wants to move ahead with the proposal submission anyway.

The veteran faculty members are counting on you to discuss the concerns as the program goes up for approval before the "Approval of New Programs" committee at the institution. You and the dean are the only two people on the committee from your academic discipline, so the others on the committee are unlikely to respond negatively. The dean is aware of your opposition to implementing the program in its current state yet assures you that she will correct any problems before the program starts. She has intimated her expectation of your giving the program your support when the "Approval of New Programs" committee meets next week. After all, she reminds you, this program needs to be implemented right away for the success of the college. If you do say something at the meeting (as your faculty colleagues are expecting you to do), it may cause other committee members to question if the program should move forward for approval.

What do you do?

_____

_____

_____

_____

_____

_____

_____

Suggested Reading: Maulding Green, W. and Leonard, E. (2019). *The Soft Skills of Leadership: Navigating with Confidence and Humility* (Second Edition). Rowman & Littlefield, Lanham, MD. Chapter 6.

Additional Selected Reading: Baur, J. E., Ellen, B. I., Buckley, M. R., Ferris, G. R., Allison, T. H., McKenny, A. F., and Short, J. C. (2016). "More Than One Way to Articulate a Vision: A Configurations Approach to Leader Charismatic Rhetoric and Influence." *The Leadership Quarterly*, 27(1), 156–171. doi:10.1016/j.leaqua.2015.08.002.

WHO IS TO BLAME?

You are a new administrator at a large state institution. The office you have inherited has a history of employee complaints and a cloud of discontent. Nonetheless, you feel confident you can turn the place around with some training and positive leadership.

One of the more challenging employees makes a public mistake. He sends an email congratulating almost a thousand students on their degree award. The problem is that these students are only sophomores. While embarrassing, it is not "mission critical." You see this as a teachable moment and more a lack of judgment than an offense that should cost him his job. The student newspaper covers the email story as does a student blog. This story is getting a lot of publicity but truly, no harm was done. You inform upper administration of the mistake and move forward.

Over the weekend, however, one upper level administrator hears a waiter joking about the email at a local eatery. She does not like the institution being the brunt of a joke. On Monday, she demands you fire the employee who sent the emails. You make a case that this action is not necessary and that the employee can be salvaged. Your boss asks if you are listening. She is not asking for your opinion; she is telling you what to do. It is your job or the "email guy's" job.

What do you do?

_____

_____

_____

_____

_____

_____

_____

Suggested Reading: Maulding Green, W. and Leonard, E. (2019). *The Soft Skills of Leadership: Navigating with Confidence and Humility* (Second Edition). Rowman & Littlefield, Lanham, MD. Chapter 6.

Additional Selected Reading: Ndalamba, K. K., Caldwell, C., and Anderson, V. (2018). "Leadership Vision as a Moral Duty." *Journal Of Management Development*, 37(3), 309–319.

THE COST OF DOING BUSINESS

In your first year as a department head you are assigned by the "committee on committees" to several committees related to your position, that is, the student activities committee. Among the other committees you are assigned to is the athletic committee.

The first time the athletic committee meets an item on the agenda is consideration of recommending to the president and board of trustees that consideration should be given to adding a football program to the athletic programs offered by the university. This item seems to come at an awkward time as the president has just announced revenue is down. This is due to a nationwide economic downturn that has impacted donations combined. This coupled with a slight drop in student enrollment means that there will be no pay raises for faculty or staff during the upcoming fiscal year. As the meeting proceeds, it is obvious that the athletic director, not surprisingly, supports this issue, yet the coaches are about evenly split. The start-up cost of the program alone is over $2,000,000, not to mention the ongoing operating costs. As discussion of the item draws to a close, a motion is made and second given to vote on the issue. It is a roll call vote. The vote is evenly split as it comes to you—yours will be the deciding vote.

How do you vote?

_____

_____

_____

_____

_____

_____

_____

Suggested Reading: Maulding Green, W. and Leonard, E. (2019). *The Soft Skills of Leadership: Navigating with Confidence and Humility* (Second Edition). Rowman & Littlefield, Lanham, MD. Chapter 6.

Additional Selected Reading: Mombourquette, C. (2017). "The Role of Vision in Effective School Leadership." *International Studies in Educational Administration (Commonwealth Council for Educational Administration & Management (CCEAM))*, 45(1), 19–36.

ONE FOR THE ROAD?

You are the associate dean. The new dean works for two weeks and then calls in sick and is out for a few days. When he returns, he says it was a reoccurrence of dengue fever he contracted years before. After several more absences, it becomes apparent he is an alcoholic.

What do you do?

_____

_____

_____

_____

_____

_____

_____

Suggested Reading: Maulding Green, W. and Leonard, E. (2019). *The Soft Skills of Leadership: Navigating with Confidence and Humility* (Second Edition). Rowman & Littlefield, Lanham, MD. Chapter 6.

Additional Selected Reading: Bonau, S. (2017). "How to Become an Inspirational Leader, and What to Avoid." *Journal of Management Development*, *36*(5), 614–625. doi:10.1108/JMD-03-2015-0047.

TAKING SIDES?

As an upper-level administrator, you have developed a package of three doctoral proposals to go before the state higher education board. You face tremendous opposition from other doctoral-granting institutions in the state. You work hard to justify the proposals and the head of the higher education board supports the proposals. You believe you will gain approval.

In a meeting with the board staff, one of the staff members negatively critiques one of the three proposals. The administrators involved with this specific proposal get defensive and want to show the staff member how wrong she is.

What do you do?

_____

_____

_____

_____

_____

_____

_____

Suggested Reading: Maulding Green, W. and Leonard, E. (2019). *The Soft Skills of Leadership: Navigating with Confidence and Humility* (Second Edition). Rowman & Littlefield, Lanham, MD. Chapter 6.

Additional Selected Reading: Strese, Steffen, Keller, Michael, Flatten, Tessa C., and Brettel, Malte. (2018). "CEOs' Passion for Inventing and Radical Innovations in SMEs: The Moderating Effect of Shared Vision." *Journal of Small Business Management*, 56(3), 435. doi:10.1111/jsbm.12264.

8

AUTHORS' OPTIONS FOR VISION SJTS

READY FOR A PROMOTION?

A. Go file an official complaint with the HR director at your institution.
B. Go to the dean and ask her to explain how you did not meet the minimum job qualifications.
C. Go to the president of the institution and explain your situation.
D. Hire an attorney and sue the institution.
E. Do nothing.
F. Other option:

_____

_____

_____

HOUSTON . . . WE HAVE A PROBLEM

A. Say nothing at the meeting and trust that your dean will fix the problems with the new program before it begins.
B. Bring up your concerns at the meeting, which could very well cause a delay or stop the program from being implemented.
C. Say nothing at the meeting, but attempt to get the veteran faculty members together and go discuss the program concerns with the academic provost.
D. Use your recent sickness as an excuse to not attend the meeting.
E. Other option:

_____

_____

_____

WHO IS TO BLAME?

A. Go to HR to be sure you have cause to fire an employee.
B. Fire the employee, it is you or him.
C. Give it a few days, perhaps clearer heads will prevail.
D. Other option:

_____

_____

_____

THE COST OF DOING BUSINESS

A. As the newest committee member, abstain from voting leaving a split vote pending input from the president and other stakeholders.
B. You are a great fan of football and think it should be added. Vote for the item.
C. The president's remarks about the budget issues linger and you vote "no."
D. Make a motion to table the item and see if you can get a second.
E. Other option:

_____

_____

_____

ONE FOR THE ROAD?

A. Confront the dean.
B. Consult with the dean's family.
C. Report the incidents to higher administration.
D. Wait it out. Some issues are best left to the observation and action of others.
E. Other option:

_____

_____

_____

TAKING SIDES?

A. Meet with the administrators and convince them overall approval of the program is much more important than trying to win an argument over a detail in the program.

B. Meet with the administrators and tell them to stop arguing with program staff.
C. Meet with the administrators and tell them that arguing with program staff is counterproductive.
D. Move on from the meeting and hope that the argumentative administrators did not derail the opportunity for new programs.
E. Other option:

_____

_____

_____

LESSONS ON EMOTIONAL INTELLIGENCE/SOFT SKILLS

Being emotionally intelligent means a lot of things. It includes the ability to recognize emotions in ourselves, controlling or regulating those emotions, acknowledging the same in others, and having a social/relationship awareness. Specifically, in the last two categories of emotional intelligence (relationship management and social awareness) fall what is currently commonly referred to as "soft skills." Additionally, with the incredible influx of technology into our lives, many of us are not nearly as "in tune" with others as in the past.

It is *critical*, now more than ever in our rapidly advancing, fast-paced society, that we give top priority to this crucial relationship-building and sustaining skill. In regard to emotional intelligence and the subsequent soft skills therein, we must ask—does the leader say what he or she means and support that with his or her actions? The answer to that question defines the soft skills of the leader.

The scenarios in this chapter are, in one way or another, related to a leader's Emotional Intelligence/Soft Skills. If your Leader Acumen assessment scores indicate this as an area for needed growth, you should work through the scenarios with a couple of things in mind. First, as you work through the scenarios in the chapter, take particular note of the *Authors' Options* to each problem at the end of each chapter of SJTs. In working through the scenarios and reviewing the *Authors' Options*, one of two things will happen. You will find disparity between your responses and the authors, or you might, indeed, find that your responses coincide with the authors' (see Appendix B for a graphic representation). Next, reflect on the information you gained from the LSI assessment. If you acknowledge that Emotional Intelligence/Soft Skills is an area for growth based on the assessment, ask yourself if this was based on your Self-assessment, the Circle assessment, or both.

If either or both assessments (the Self or Circle) indicate that you have room for improvement in the area of leader Competence *and* you are also finding disparity in yours and the *Authors' Options*, chances are you will find growth via working through these exercises and accompanying readings. However, be reminded, this will not happen overnight. Growing your *Leader Acumen* is a worthy endeavor but is a painstakingly time-consuming undertaking. It requires rewiring of your thought processes regarding learnings that are very much ingrained into your most innate thought processes and this takes time (see Appendix B for a graphic representation).

On the other hand, if you find your solutions and the solutions offered in the *Authors' Options* coincide highly, yet your Self score is lower than the mean shown at the end of your LSI assessment for Emotional Intelligence/Soft Skills, one of two things is happening. Either you are lacking in self-confidence, yet your decision-making is solid, or perhaps you are somewhat overconfident but nonetheless making good decisions. If the first is the case, working through the scenarios should enhance your self-confidence. The second option (overconfidence) is the one to be most wary of. Leaders in this category, many times find themselves derailed as leaders, even though they generally are good decision makers. Working through the scenarios should help in instilling the idea that there is more than one acceptable solution to most problem/issues and thus lessen one potential major consequence of overconfidence, feeling that you have the only viable solution.

If you opt to have a Circle/360-assessment done and find that your solutions and the solutions offered in the *Authors' Options* coincide highly, yet your Circle scores were outside the standard deviation (available from the LEAD team when a Circle/360-assessment is done) LSI for Emotional Intelligence/Soft Skills, it is possible that a different set of problems is occurring. Either you are selecting the course of action you believe is best for the scenario, yet in reality you would not implement it, or the problem may be one of *perception*. It is much more likely that it is the former. Only in rare instances would the latter be the case. However, we insert it here for thought because, on occasion, it is the case. And, as the old saying goes, perception is reality.

Perhaps you do indeed have good soft skills yet *perception* is the issue for your low scores in Emotional Intelligence/Soft Skills. This could be a case of projection. For example, you may not seem emotionally intelligent (or to have good soft skills) and perhaps for legitimate reasons. You will recall from the chapter on credibility in *Leadership Intelligence: Navigating to Your True North* that mention was made of how "what you wear" infers or projects an image. Such could be the case in this instance.

Finally, improving your Leader Acumen and "adaptive capacity," as stated in the preface, is a process. As you will recall, the notion of Leader Acumen is predicated on the theory that there is a genetic predisposition toward leadership.

As Marquis and Tilscik[1] so aptly noted, imprinting may take place, during brief sensitive periods of high susceptibility during the formative process, during the teachable moment or another yet different time of susceptibility, and that imprints once established are persistent.

The lessons in this book are to be utilized to grow Leader Acumen in this third way—over the long, repetitive process. To that end and to truly be imprinted with any of the competencies, actions for building the various skillsets may be found in Appendix C.

"The leader who, through developing his/her leader acumen, can also master the ability to recognize and react appropriately to both the rational and emotional sides of an individual has a decided advantage over the leader who lacks those abilities."[2]

A BUMPY ROAD

You are an experienced mid-level financial manager in a large university. You have six administrative departments under your supervision. In each department, there is a department head and numerous employees.

With the impending retirement of one of your department heads approaching, you take applications for a suitable replacement. After interviews are completed, you select the candidate that looks to be the most qualified and appoint him to the position. The successful candidate is an existing employee in one of your other departments and has an excellent work record. Although this person has never been a supervisor before, he has demonstrated his potential for higher responsibilities. You make sure this new department head has the opportunity to work with the retiring department head for a couple of weeks to ensure a smooth transition.

About a month after the new department head has been in charge of this department, you begin to receive complaints from employees about the way he runs the department. The complaints have a common theme—they say he is bossy, abrupt, and domineering. You have worked with and known this person for years and these comments do not fit with your past experiences with him. Also, this has been a smooth operating department with a number of experienced employees for a long time and the only thing that changed was the appointment of a new department head.

_____

_____

_____

_____

_____

_____

_____

Suggested Reading: Maulding Green, W. and Leonard, E. (2019). *The Soft Skills of Leadership: Navigating with Confidence and Humility* (Second Edition). Rowman & Littlefield, Lanham, MD. Chapter 7.

Additional Selected Reading: Phipps, S. A. and Prieto, L. C. (2017). "Why Emotional Intelligence Is Necessary for Effective Leadership: Know the Four Reasons!" *Leadership Excellence Essentials*, 34(6), 56.

LEADERSHIP = HEARTBURN

There may be nothing more important for college of education administrators to deal with other than issues impacting accreditation. Without accreditation from regional associations, such as SACS, degrees are useless as state agencies will not grant licenses for students with diplomas from unaccredited universities. Consequently, students could have educational loans that they can never pay off. Parents may become vocal and begin complaining to upper level administrators and even the press as they feel their children have wasted their time. Local school districts may not be able to fill teaching vacancies, and enrollment at the university may drastically decline.

You are currently chair of one of the departments in the college. Although matters pertaining to the department are going well, two years into your tenure as chair, the college's accrediting agency conducts a site visit and does not renew the college's accreditation. Because of potentially devastating consequences, the president decides to replace the dean and asks if you would be willing to serve in that capacity. The current dean is popular among tenured professors in the college, and you are reluctant to agree. But after reflection you decide to accept the position.

After you begin working in this new capacity, you find out that the president does not want to announce the reason why the dean was replaced because of the potentially negative impact that news would have on enrollment. Faculty then become outraged accusing the president of making the change of leadership because of "dirty politics" and their perceived friendship the president has with you. You are bewildered as you are not from the area, have only known the president for a few years, and have had no social interaction with him or anyone in his family. Eventually, the faculty senate becomes involved and some professors begin pressuring you to resign.

Regardless, during the ensuing time period, you have worked with your leadership team and have addressed the college's deficiencies. As a result of this effort, the college is able to secure full accreditation once again. Nonetheless, the full professors are still belligerent toward you and uncooperative.

What do you do?

_____
_____
_____
_____
_____

Suggested Reading: Maulding Green, W. and Leonard, E. (2019). *The Soft Skills of Leadership: Navigating with Confidence and Humility* (Second Edition). Rowman & Littlefield, Lanham, MD. Chapter 7.

Additional Selected Reading: McCarroll, J. (2018). "SOFT SKILLS Have Never Been so Important." *NZ Business + Management*, *32*(6), M14–M15.

INSIDER INFORMATION

You are a professor at a university. You work in graduate programs that serve many working professionals earning advanced graduate degrees. Among these professionals earning advanced degrees are faculty and staff from surrounding vocational, technical, and two-year institutions.

You happen to serve on the board of trustees at one of these surrounding two-year institutions, so you teach several students who also work at the institution in which you serve as a board member. Lately, there have been a lot of problems at the institution where you serve as a board member. In particular, many employees at the two-year institution, who are also your students, are very unhappy with the administration at their school. These students know you are a board member at their institution, so they discuss with you the problems and issues occurring. Several of them have valid complaints.

Administration at your university encourages good, positive relationships with all surrounding vocational, technical, and two-year schools because students from these schools often transfer to your institution. Still, you are aware of some unacceptable issues occurring at the two-year institution, which could cause problems if not addressed. While there are several issues, the most pressing seems to be the abuse of power of the executive head and cabinet, and how the structure and rules of the two-year institution can change on a daily basis.

While other board members seem to understand that there might be some unhappy employees and other minor problems at the two-year institution, they do not have the "inside information" to which you are privy. You want to help those employees at the two-year institution, but you also understand that a wrong move could be disastrous on many levels and have negative repercussions.

What do you do?

_____

_____

_____

_____

_____

_____

_____

Suggested Reading: Maulding Green, W. and Leonard, E. (2019). *The Soft Skills of Leadership: Navigating with Confidence and Humility* (Second Edition). Rowman & Littlefield, Lanham, MD. Chapter 7.

Additional Selected Reading: Goleman, D. and Lippincott, M. (2017). "Without Emotional Intelligence, Mindfulness Doesn't Work." *Harvard Business School Cases*, 2017, 1.

TASTY TREATS?

It all began at the reception for the visiting Greek ambassador. The university was notified that the Greek ambassador wished to visit, tour the campus, and meet with the university leadership. A grand reception was planned as the culminating activity and you, as planning associate in the Office of Planning and Institutional Research, were invited to attend. Prior to the reception, all were informed that the ambassador had limited English skills, so no long conversations—just smiles and pleasantries were the order of the day. There would be a formal reception line, brief conversations, and refreshments. All was in order. The room was lovely, flowers perfect, refreshments placed, and the city view enhanced the whole affair. Nothing would foretell how unique your experiences that evening would be.

It started in the reception line. As the reception line formed, you note that one of the institution's premier research professors had somehow forgotten to "zip up." (He may have had a cocktail or two for lunch.) Not only that, his belt had been tightened in such a way as to pull the flap back. Something had to be done! So, you slip over to the executive vice president and provost, a distinguished and religious man, and asked him to "Do Something!" He notes the problem, smiled slightly, chuckles, and asked if you often checked men's zippers as you traverse through receiving lines. You turn crimson. The professor disappears from the reception.

You move quickly into the reception area and you happen upon the president, a brilliant man. He is a very large former Alabama football player with a Harvard law degree and had been president of the university for about thirty years. Rumor had it he was on the hunt for an executive assistant. As brilliant as he was, it was also well known that he could be quite unusual, a hard taskmaster, and had other unexpected behaviors (gossip suggested that he had sent the mail cart through a glass door as well as taken men's ties that he had admired). "Ah ha," the president said, "So good to see you today. I was just thinking about you as I am in dire need of an outstanding Executive Assistant. Please start immediately working in my office."

You explain to him that you have two teenage children who need your time and attention and also that you are well pleased to be working as a planning associate in the Office of Planning and Institutional Research. The president is aware that you have served as an academic administrator at another institution and tells you that his preference for having a "low-profile" job will not be to your benefit at the university.

At this point he indicates (in a commanding voice) that while he was serving in World War II in New Guinea, the island rats used to try to maintain a "low profile" and that he would mow them down in his jeep. At this point, your head is swimming and you tell him perhaps you can discuss things later. At this, he responds by indicating that the two of you should slip out of the reception and go to his office for a resolution to the issue.

It is at this point that the strange really gets stranger. As you leave the reception, the president fills all his pockets with six or seven canned soft drinks and orders you to take a large platter of cookies and canapés. Off you set for his office. After he polishes off most of the treats and numerous beverages, you have a pleasant conversation with nothing decided. The plan is to continue the conversation the next day. You flee to your office.

After breathing a sigh of relief, the associate provost comes into the office and informs you that you are in a lot of trouble! You were seen carrying the cookies and canapés from the reception to the office of the president. Did you not know that the office that pays for the reception keeps the remaining goodies for their staff? You had absconded with the provost's goodies! This was an unpardonable offense!

What should you do?

_____

_____

_____

_____

_____

_____

_____

Suggested Reading: Maulding Green, W. and Leonard, E. (2019). *The Soft Skills of Leadership: Navigating with Confidence and Humility* (Second Edition). Rowman & Littlefield, Lanham, MD. Chapter 7.

Additional Selected Reading: McKee, A. (2016). "How the Most Emotionally Intelligent CEOs Handle Their Power." *Harvard Business School Cases*, 2016, 1.

A WORD TO THE WISE

A new department head for the Student Assistance area has joined the Student Service Department where you serve as director of student life. He is amicable and a personable young man but is obviously not accustomed to a prominent leadership role and tends to be directive in his approach. A longtime friend/colleague of yours works in his department. Over the time your friend and you have been at the university you have made a habit of sharing your coffee break on a regular basis (but not every day) as work varies each of your schedules.

About a month into the new department head's tenure, your supervisor calls to say that she needs to speak with you. Nothing unusual about her call, as she calls frequently to ask you to come speak with her. When you arrive at her office, though, it is obvious that she is upset. After brief pleasantries, she tells you that the new department head has filed a complaint against you. The new department head says you are taking up too much of your friend's time and he wants you to stop visiting your friend so frequently. You explain to your supervisor when and how often you visit. This information, of course, she already knows as she keeps a close eye on the department. She shares with you that while she does not think you are interfering with your friend's work, she would like for you to "set things right" with the new department head for the sake of the smooth functioning of the department.

What do you do?

_____

_____

_____

_____

_____

_____

_____

Suggested Reading: Maulding Green, W. and Leonard, E. (2019). *The Soft Skills of Leadership: Navigating with Confidence and Humility* (Second Edition). Rowman & Littlefield, Lanham, MD. Chapter 7.

Additional Selected Reading: McKee, A. (2016). "If You Can't Empathize with Your Employees, You'd Better Learn to." *Harvard Business Review Digital Articles*, 2016, 2–5.

INTERNATIONAL STUDENT DILEMMA

Your university has a bankruptcy policy. Students can have their previous academic record erased and start over. The handbook has one disclaimer: any student who declares bankruptcy cannot earn "honors" no matter what their GPA after bankruptcy.

An international student declares bankruptcy and then earns a 4.00 GPA. His parents come for graduation expecting him to graduate "with honors." His home country makes his level of employment dependent on graduation "with honors." When the student finds out he will not graduate "with honors," he is devastated. He has dishonored his parents and is trapped in a lower-status job for life. He asks you to waive the rule and let him graduate "with honors."

What do you do?

_____

_____

_____

_____

_____

_____

_____

Suggested Reading: Maulding Green, W. and Leonard, E. (2019). *The Soft Skills of Leadership: Navigating with Confidence and Humility* (Second Edition). Rowman & Littlefield, Lanham, MD. Chapter 7.

Additional Selected Reading: Goleman, D. and Boyatzis, R. E. (2017). "Emotional Intelligence Has 12 Elements. Which Do You Need to Work On?" *Harvard Business Review Digital Articles*, 2017, 2–5.

CLEARING THE AIR

As vice president, one of your senior administrators is known to be unhappy with you. She is an older, longtime employee. She comes to your office in tears and asks, "Why don't you like me?" It turns out she is upset because you do not give her hugs as her previous bosses and other administrators do.

What do you do?

_____

_____

_____

_____

_____

_____

_____

Suggested Reading: Maulding Green, W. and Leonard, E. (2019). *The Soft Skills of Leadership: Navigating with Confidence and Humility* (Second Edition). Rowman & Littlefield, Lanham, MD. Chapter 7.

Additional Selected Reading: Goleman, D. (2017). "Here's What Mindfulness Is (and Isn't) Good For." *Harvard Business Review Digital Articles*, 2017, 2–4.

A DAY'S PAY FOR A DAY'S WORK

As a senior administrator, your secretary is at the top of her pay scale as a Secretary Level 4 on the pay scale. The only way to get her a substantial pay raise is to make her into an administrative assistant (which is a rank above Secretary Level 4). The work she performs is that of a Secretary Level 4 and not that of an administrative assistant.

What do you do?

_____
_____
_____
_____
_____
_____
_____

Suggested Reading: Maulding Green, W. and Leonard, E. (2019). *The Soft Skills of Leadership: Navigating with Confidence and Humility* (Second Edition). Rowman & Littlefield, Lanham, MD. Chapter 7.

Additional Selected Reading: Carucci, R. (2018). "Is Your Emotional Intelligence Authentic, or Self-Serving?" *Harvard Business Review Digital Articles*, 2018, 2–5.

WORKING IT OUT

You have been hired as the department head of an administrative department in a large university. Although you have a lot of experience in this type of work, this is your first time to manage other employees. In your department, you are responsible for managing the activities of eight people. You accepted the position knowing that the department is barely staffed to get the current workload done. Additionally, your department has many critical deadlines to meet in the ordinary conduct of its business.

About two weeks after you start in your new role, one of your most valuable employees has an accident and breaks her leg. Because she has a full leg cast, she cannot drive and cannot come to the office. This is an employee that you feel you cannot do without. Other than the fact that she is not able to get to work and that she could not sit at a desk all day if she was there, the employee is capable of doing her work. She also wants to work because she has no sick leave time accumulated and she needs her paycheck.

It is commonly understood that the institution does not have a work-from-home policy, so you have to figure out how to get the work done and meet the required fixed deadlines. This is a payroll department and not meeting the deadlines is not an option! People would not get their paychecks and a possibly chaotic situation could develop. You are responsible.

What do you do?

_____

_____

_____

_____

_____

_____

_____

_____

Suggested Reading: Maulding Green, W. and Leonard, E. (2019). *The Soft Skills of Leadership: Navigating with Confidence and Humility* (Second Edition). Rowman & Littlefield, Lanham, MD. Chapter 7.

Additional Selected Reading: Benjamin, B. (2018). "The Resurgence of Emotional Intelligence: Six Reasons Why EQ Matters More Than Ever." *Leadership Excellence Essentials*, *35*(3), 21.

10

AUTHORS' OPTIONS FOR EMOTIONAL INTELLIGENCE SJTS

A BUMPY ROAD

A. Do nothing and hope that things will settle down as the new department head gains more experience.

B. Call the department head in and tell him about the multiple employee complaints about his management style. You tell him the department has been running successfully for a long time and the only thing that changed was the supervisor. In baseball, when the ball is not going through the Strike Zone, the manager does not come out to replace the ball. Under the university's rules, he is an "at will" employee and can be terminated immediately. You give him a strong warning and a short time to remedy the situation.

C. You call the department head in as in point B, but you do not give him a strong warning. Instead you tell him about the complaints and have a counseling session with him to try to determine why he was not being successful in his new role.

D. Other option:

_____

_____

_____

LEADERSHIP = HEARTBURN

A. Tell your faculty the reason why the president moved you into the dean's position.

B. Continue to keep this secret and work to dismiss the professors who are being belligerent and uncooperative by eliminating their travel and operational budgets.

C. Send an application to every university in the country with a dean vacancy.

D. Sit tight and wait for the belligerent and uncooperative professors to retire.

E. Work on building a positive relationship with those who are belligerent and uncooperative.

F. Ask the president to talk to the faculty and explain the entire situation.

G. Other option:

_____

_____

_____

INSIDER INFORMATION

A. Do nothing so you will not cause problems between your institution and the two-year institution and its employees.

B. Discuss the concerns formally at the next board meeting with the executive head and the other board members.

C. Have some private conversations with a couple of other board members that you trust about the issues of which you are aware.

D. Discuss the issues of which you are aware with your colleagues to see if they can offer any advice.

E. Other option:

_____

_____

_____

TASTY TREATS?

A. Write a note of apology to the provost and send an appropriate edible gift reparation.

B. Call on the president to intervene.

C. Revise your vitae in case it is a serious infraction.

D. Seek advice from colleagues.

E. Other option:

_____

_____

_____

A WORD TO THE WISE

A. Call the new department head and tell him you will be visiting your friend less frequently but that you did not appreciate him going to your supervisor.

B. Tell your friend/colleague why, and then visit less frequently but say nothing to the new department head.

C. On further consideration, the fact the new department head has filed a complaint against you has irritated you tremendously. Go see the new department head and tell him just what you think of his cowardly actions.

D. Go see the new department head and tell him you had no intention to interfere with his department in any way and that you will visit less often and make the visits shorter.

E. Other option:

_____

_____

_____

INTERNATIONAL STUDENT DILEMMA

A. Make an exception.

B. Enforce the rule.

C. Seek a change to the rule.

D. Write a letter to the student's parents and government officials.

E. Other option:

_____

_____

_____

CLEARING THE AIR

A. Explain that you are not a person given to physical expression of satisfaction with a person's work.

B. Explain that what others do is up to them but that you are not a person given to physical expression of satisfaction with a person's work.

C. Explain that not hugging has nothing to do with liking or not liking her.

D. Explain the realities of sexual harassment in the current climate while assuring her of my respect for her work.

E. Other option:

_____

_____

_____

A DAY'S PAY FOR A DAY'S WORK

A. Make the change to help your secretary.
B. Do not make the undeserved change in title.
C. Postpone any decision to see what other administrators do.
D. Explain to her why you will not make the change.
E. Other option:

_____

_____

_____

WORKING IT OUT

A. Go to your supervisor and ask him or her what to do and let him or her make the decision because of the significance of the problem.
B. Go about your regular schedule and hope you meet the payroll deadline.
C. Take two anxiety pills and mellow out.
D. Write out a strongly written request to your supervisor to do the following: Approve an immediate exception to the work-from-home policy for this employee for the duration of her recuperation. This would be welcome to the employee because of her indicated desire to work from home and her lack of accumulated sick leave. Additionally, you should try hard to convince your supervisor of the importance of this solution. This should be done in person, not just by a written memorandum or email.
E. Take it upon yourself to deliver her work to her at home each day.
F. Alert the other employees about the possibility of working overtime to meet deadlines.
G. Other option:

_____

_____

_____

AUTHORS' SOLUTIONS FOR SJTS

Disclaimer: In the following pages are the authors' recommended solutions, rationale, and reasoning for rejection of alternative solutions. These recommendations are in no way intended to supersede work policy or act as legal advice to the learner. These are actual situations encountered by the authors including the solutions they enacted at the time and place of the circumstance.

AUTHORS' SOLUTIONS: CREDIBILITY

CLINICAL TRIALS AND TRIBULATIONS

Best Solution: B—Tell the faculty members (instructor and chair) that the university policy requires that they allow the student to make up the missed coursework and that you will ensure that they abide by this policy.

Rationale for Best Solution: Sometimes you just have to require and clearly state that we must follow the prescribed policy as it is fair and ethical.

Rationale for Rejecting the Alternate Solutions

A. This may feel like the "easy" option in your role, but it is not ethical nor is it the right thing to do since it is clear that the faculty members are not abiding by policy and appear to be discriminating against the student.

C. This is not ideal as a grievance is not productive when we have a policy to prevent this behavior.

D. This is not productive and will come across as snarky and unprofessional.

EXAM TIME

Best Solution: B—Point out the great strides that have been made.

Rationale for Best Solution: It is always a good idea to present a balanced picture if for no other reason than future reference.

Rationale for Rejecting the Alternate Solutions

A. Saying nothing is tantamount to an admission of malfeasance.

C. Threats are never a good starting point as the threats are usually met with hostility. And—remember you are dealing with someone in a superior position.

D. There is a time for this step. This is not it. It is best to leave on a good note, if possible.

DECISIONS, DECISIONS

Best Solution: A—If you got it in writing, you have a case.

Rationale for Best Solution: When changing positions within an organization and/or moving to a new position in a new organization, it is wise to protect yourself by putting any employment stipulations in writing.

Rationale for Rejecting the Alternate Solutions

B. This may become a consideration if other paths do not resolve the situation, but it is not a good first step.

C. This could also be a necessary step but should not be the first step.

D. There is a time for this step. This is not it. It is best to leave on a good note, if possible.

THE END JUSTIFIES THE MEANS

Best Response: A—Go talk to the IRB administrator/chair and make him/her aware of the situation.

Rationale for Best Solution: The IRB administrator and chair will know what to do since they have training and expertise in this area. You can ask him or her to not disclose your identity, but it could become necessary as he or she begins to investigate.

Rationale for Rejecting the Alternate Responses

B. This option is not bad, but it is not appropriate since this is not the dean's area of expertise. It could, possibly, make the dean think that you are trying to create issues for your colleagues.

C. While you could do this, it is probably not wise to do so without concrete proof. Also, the chain of command should be respected and that would include going to your IRB chair/administrator. The IRB chair/administrator will know how to handle the situation.

D. Not very wise to keep quiet, especially since so much is on the line—including human subjects' protection and loss of institutional status to compete for grants.

POINT OF VIEW

Best Solution: B—Tell the father that you appreciate his concern and hope that the threat is the end of the situation but that you did not implicate his son. Furthermore, he should do as he deems best from a legal point of view.

Rationale for Best Solution: Expressing concern is a genuine expression in this situation, given the alleged threat. However, since the allegations about your behavior are untrue you should stand your ground.

Rationale for Rejecting the Alternate Solutions

A. This amounts to only a partial and insensitive response as it does not address the potential for harm from the threats to his son.

C. Allowing the president to respond is tempting but not appropriate as he was not privy to all of the details of the investigation leading to the dismissal.

D. No apology is need as you acted correctly and saying more simply antagonizes the parent.

CANDID CAMERA

Best Solution: C—Do some research to make sure you know the verbiage and then call in the students one by one keeping them separated and confront each one.

Rationale for Best Solution: There is sufficient evidence on the tape to warrant further investigation. But it is always best to know what you are talking about/ viewing.

Rationale for Rejecting the Alternate Solutions

A. A tempting solution but student discipline is your area of responsibility.

B. This may be a necessary step but not the first step.

D. Inaction will become known and will undermine your credibility.

AUTHORS' SOLUTIONS: COMPETENCE

PRACTICE WHAT YOU PREACH

Best Response: B—Tell the academic records specialist that this was not something she was allowed to do because the student was from a different college, ask that she apologize to the advisor, and that she never does this again.

Rationale for Best Solution: The academic records specialist had no authority to remove a student from a different college from the course. Her actions put another university employee in a difficult situation and the student's requirements would not be met that particular semester without the freshman year experience course.

Rationale for Rejecting the Alternate Responses

A. While you want the academic records specialist to assist all students at the university, she must understand the scope of her role.

C. This option would not be ideal as it puts the student in an awkward position. She needs the course and was told by her family friend that she did not need it. She may feel as though she is getting her friend in trouble.

D. Administrators should only defend employees who have done the right thing in the situation.

THE GOOD, THE BAD, AND THE UGLY

Best Solution: C—Take no action but continue doing the best job as possible given the circumstances.

Rationale for Best Solution: Talking to the dean will be a fruitless endeavor, as past discussions have led to nowhere. Talking with others will probably yield similar results, or worse. Continue working hard and making a positive impact where you can and wait for an opportunity to move to a better situation.

Rationales for Rejecting the Alternate Solutions

A. This is not going to work because the dean does not want anyone "to rock the boat" and possibly tarnish her image and impede her quest to advance. Her action will continue to be a lack of action.
B. Talking to the provost might help, but it could also make things worse for you and your colleagues. What if the provost divulges your identity to the dean? If the dean is a type to hold a grudge, then it could be even worse if she gets promoted.
C. Talking to the other deans might give you some good ideas, but once again, what if someone divulges your identity? This would, more than likely, upset the dean because you have tarnished her image.

THE EMBATTLED DEAN

Best Solution: C—Meet with the entire faculty, listening to both critics and supporters of the dean and offering confidential meetings for faculty members who are reluctant to speak publicly.

Rationale for Best Solution: You should determine whether the attitude of the faculty members who supported the "no confidence" vote is widespread among the faculty at large. Because nontenured faculty may fear retaliation from either the college administration or the senior faculty who oppose the dean, they should be given an opportunity to express themselves in confidence. Similarly, some supporters of the dean among the tenured faculty may have been reluctant to get involved in the conflict between the dean and his or her critics. Your follow-up actions should be driven by the results of the investigation. Simultaneously, you should assure the donors that both faculty and administration will continue to carry out the mission of the college in a professional manner.

Rationale for Rejecting the Alternate Solutions

A. Notwithstanding your long friendship with the dean, you have an obligation to take the expressed concerns seriously and investigate them before taking action.
B. While you are justifiably concerned about the potential impacts of the "no confidence" resolution and negative publicity on donor support, the faculty members

who oppose the dean likely will take your position as blind support for your personal friend and disregard for their concerns.

D. Presumably the faculty has participated in a confidential performance review of the dean within the past year. If these concerns were not generally expressed in that process, you may want to determine what circumstances may have changed since then to generate a call for the dean's removal.

WHAT DID YOU SAY?

Best Solution: D—Dismiss the committee and ask the provost to stay and speak to you privately. Express your concerns about potential policy and due process violations and tell him that he will have to put in writing his directive to dismiss the student.

Rationale for Best Solution: Higher authority, even when wrong, can force an action. Nonetheless, it is imperative to establish a paper trail of responsibility to have in the event of legal action.

Rationale for Rejecting the Alternate Solutions

A. Simply acquiescing to the provost, while expedient, does not address the potential legal issues of not following due process.

B. Arguing with the provost in front of the committee is unprofessional.

C. Threatening to go over the provost's head is also unprofessional, though at some point it might be a step you have to take.

CHOICES, CHOICES

Best Solution: A—Thoroughly research the background of the former head coach to be comfortable he will not undermine you, and hire him or her.

Rationale for Best Solution: The best decisions are made with the best information. You are the decision maker. Having someone with more information than you and your young staff possess is good.

Rationale for Rejecting the Alternate Solutions

B. This action deprives you of the knowledge of the experienced coach.

C. This may pay dividends but essentially just delays the choice.

AND THE FINAL SCORE IS?

> **Best Solution:** B—Meet with the staff who are responsible for the reviews and discuss making the reviews more meaningful.
>
> **Rationale for Best Solution:** Problem issues are best resolved through open discussion and feedback.

Rationale for Rejecting the Alternate Solutions

A. This may be tempting but in essence substitutes your judgment for the reviewers.

C. This may be tempting but in essence substitutes your judgment for the reviewers and will probably alienate the reviewers.

D. This too is temping but in essence undermines your relationship with the reviewers.

Author's note: I asked for feedback but dropped the subject in light of overwhelming opposition.

BLOWING IN THE WIND

> **Best Solution:** B—Act according to the prescribed procedure for a student on probation.
>
> **Rationale for Best Solution:** Following procedure even if overruled at some point should always be the first option.

Rationale for Rejecting the Alternate Solutions

A. If her connections intercede it should be after you have acted not before.

C. This is your area of responsibility. Keeping your supervisor informed of potential issues is correct but the decision should be yours.

D. These incidents are mild and this could be potential solution but she is on probation and been told she would be dismissed.

AUTHORS' SOLUTIONS: ABILITY TO INSPIRE

FACT OR FICTION?

Best Solution: A—Discuss your concerns with the institution's vice president of accreditation.

Rationale for Best Solution: While you should trust that the dean will fix the problem as she stated, you have no reason to believe she will because it has been several months and she has not done so yet. It would be wise to have a record of this conversation with the dean so you can report this information to the vice president of accreditation. That way, if (more than likely when) there are problems with accreditation, then you have records that you made efforts to address the problems of which you had knowledge.

Rationale for Rejecting the Alternate Solutions

B. Doing this option would probably cause tension and uneasiness for faculty, especially given some faculty have already discussed their concerns with the dean. The tension and uneasiness would be worthwhile if it would result in the problem being addressed. However, this is not likely, given the chair's and dean's past behaviors.

C. Doing nothing would be the easiest option, but you know that an institution losing its accreditation is a very serious matter. You cannot stand by and not take action.

D. This is the "nuclear" option. If you do this, it will not only get your institution in trouble, but you will find yourself out of a job very soon and most likely unemployable thereafter.

FOOTBALL FRENZY

Best Solution: E—Assure the trustees that consideration of football is a high priority for you and that when you and the administrative team have exercised due diligence to determine if the timing is right to consider football, you will recommend to the board that a comprehensive feasibility study be undertaken.

Rationale for Best Solution: A confrontation with key trustees this early in your tenure is difficult, but you must assert strongly that the decision to start any expensive new program should be done deliberately and collaboratively with all university stakeholders—trustees, students, faculty, alumni, supporters, and community leaders. Among other factors, the study would include market analysis, costs, impact on academics and student life, and support from internal and external stakeholders.

Rational for Rejecting the Alternate Solutions

A. Especially as a new president, you cannot dismiss the wishes of two key trustees out of hand. However, you should explain diplomatically that it would be irresponsible of you to recommend an expensive new program without having devoted adequate time to assess the university's financial condition and to gauge support from all stakeholders.

B. Placing the matter on the agenda as proposed by the trustees implies a level of analysis and endorsement on the part of the administration that has not occurred. Although the trustees on their own can raise the issue for discussion as "new business," you should try to convince them that public discussion of football at this time is premature and might actually harm the prospects of approving the program in the near future.

C. It would be very risky at this early stage to seek a resolution on football from faculty leaders who are skeptical of the costs and impact of the program on academics.

D. While the athletics director will play a critical role in the assessment process, the ultimate responsibility for presenting a proposal to the board falls on the president.

TIME IS NOT LIMITLESS

Best Solution: C—Discuss the situation with your supervisor and recommend that a policy be adopted.

Rationale for Best Solution: Some issues simply must be addressed by those in higher authority.

Rationale for Rejecting the Alternate Solutions

A. With no policy in place you would be overstepping your authority.
B. A sensible possible alternative but it only delays final action.
D. Standing pat will not resolve the situation.

THE TRUTH AND NOTHING BUT THE TRUTH

Best Solution: C—Follow the published handbook and do not tell him.
Rationale for Best Solution: It is not fair to others and could result in legal issues.

Rationale for Rejecting the Alternate Solutions

A. This action clearly circumvents the rule. And, it is speculation that he might become privy to the information.
B. Referring him to a higher authority is tantamount to shirking your duty. He may appeal to the higher authority but it should not be on your recommendation.
D. This is potentially a good after the fact step to take if you feel the rule is inappropriate but does nothing to address the current issue.

Author's note: As it turned out it was a good decision because he sued. I did not like having to follow the process but it was the right thing to do.

A VOICE IN THE WILDERNESS

Best Solution: B—Find the people who are supportive and develop the new PhD program.
Rationale for Best Solution: If you believe the program has merit find and develop support for it.

Rationale for Rejecting the Alternate Solutions

A. Selling an idea is part of a leader's job and this step may be taken at some point but is not the best first step.
C. There are situations in which this would be a good step but if you believe the program stopping the momentum it needs to be accepted is a misstep.
D. While this could be done, unilateral decisions of this magnitude place you in an awkward and potentially adversarial position with the entire faculty.

THE ROAD LESS TRAVELED

Best Solution: D—Convince the Senate and administrators to change to the variable job description.

Rationale for Best Solution: Change is best brought about by selling new ideas.

Rationale for Rejecting the Alternate Solutions

A. Unilateral decisions are necessary at times but not the best way resolve problems that numerous employees.
B. This is tempting but leaves a critical issue unresolved.
C. Passing problems up the line is always tempting but taking the initiative is what good leaders do.

Author's note: The process works very well for those who use it correctly.

AUTHORS' SOLUTIONS: VISION

READY FOR A PROMOTION?

Best Response: E—Do nothing.

Rationale: Sometimes you just have to rise above the fray. The dean and her cronies are going to do what they are going to do; you should exhibit class and move on. If you ever want to get out of this toxic environment (and you should), you will need some good references. Those references will be difficult to obtain if you complain and cause trouble.

Rationale for Rejecting the Alternate Solutions

A. While this seems reasonable, the dean and her chosen ones will wreak havoc on you once you have filed an official complaint. Your life will definitely be miserable.

B. This option is not bad, but what good would come out of it? As the saying goes, it would be like pouring water on a duck's back. At worst, it would cause the dean to have more animosity toward you because you questioned her.

C. Presidents usually do not get involved with hiring decisions. Also, they are usually, at least to some extent, unaware of many problems at departmental and school levels. The president could very well perceive you to be a troublemaker since you have only been at the institution for four years.

D. Yes, you very well could win the lawsuit, but it would be very difficult finding employment at another institution once you have a lawsuit under your belt.

HOUSTON . . . WE HAVE A PROBLEM

Best Solution: A—Say nothing at the meeting and trust that your dean will fix the problems with program before it begins.

Rationale for Best Solution: Even though the dean is in a new position with a lack of higher education experience, you should trust that she will fix the problems before program implementation, as promised. It would be wise to make a note of her promise to fix the problems and report this information back to the other veteran faculty. That way, if there are major problems with the program, then you or the other veteran faculty members cannot be held responsible.

Rationale for Rejecting the Alternate Solutions

B. This option would probably cause the dean to have animosity toward you because you questioned her. This could be problematic, especially if she gains more power in her quest to move up in your institution.

C. This option would cause a lack of trust between the new dean and the veteran faculty of the school. Even though she is not listening to your concerns, going over her head will make her even less willing to listen to you than she currently does. In other words, this makes a bad situation even worse.

D. While this option is not bad, how would the dean perceive you not attending the committee meeting? Could she possibly interpret this as having control over you? Would this open the door for the dean to respect your experience and opinion even less than she does now? Perhaps this will make her think you will not participate in such processes and decisions, thus allowing her to make big decisions without any input.

WHO IS TO BLAME?

Best Solution: A—Always check with HR.

Rationale for Best Solution: Ensuring that accepted policy and procedure are followed by checking with HR is a very good first step. It can prevent a suit for unlawful termination.

Rationale for Rejecting the Alternate Solutions

B. This may be the eventual outcome but acting under color of law (by accepted policy and procedure) is a better first step.

C. Inaction will probably only exacerbate the situation. It is better to seek the advice you need as a first step.

THE COST OF DOING BUSINESS

Best Solution: A—As the newest committee member, abstain from voting leaving a split vote pending input for the president and other stakeholders.

Rationale for Best Solution: This is a major step and should be vetted completely before moving forward.

Rationale for Rejecting the Alternate Solutions

B. Fan or not, if your support is genuine, vote yes, but as you have misgivings voting yes is not a good idea.
C. Voting no based on those brief remarks is a possible solution but puts the onus of voting the program down on you.
D. Robert's rules of order will not allow this.

ONE FOR THE ROAD?

Best Solution: D—Wait it out. Some issues are best left to the observation and action of others.

Rationale for Best Solution: The problem was serious enough it became obvious to senior faculty.

Rationale for Rejecting the Alternate Solutions

A. Confronting your boss (superior on the organizational chart) is problematic at best unless you have an extremely close personal relationship that allows for open discussion of what is a highly personal issue.
B. Bringing others, especially those outside the workplace, into a work-related situation may seem like a helpful gesture but is not appropriate.
C. Without definitive proof this is a bad idea.

TAKING SIDES?

Best Solution: A—Meet with the administrators and convince them that overall approval of the program is much more important than trying to win an argument over a detail in the program.

Rationale for Best Solution: The object is to secure the program. Once in place, the negative points raised can be addressed.

Rationale for Rejecting the Alternate Solutions

B. Telling your supporters not to argue is a good step but stops short of providing a rationale for not arguing.

C. Telling your supporters not to argue is a good step and providing a rationale for not arguing is better but the rationale lacks supporting detail.

D. Saying nothing invites/sanctions the behavior happening again and is not a good step.

Author's note: Doctoral programs were approved.

AUTHORS' SOLUTIONS: EMOTIONAL INTELLIGENCE/SOFT SKILLS

A BUMPY ROAD

Best Solution: C—You call the department head in but do not give him a strong warning. Instead you tell him about the complaints and have a counseling session with him to try to determine why he was not being successful in his new role.

Rationale for Best Solution: Having a frank conversation with the new appointee gives him the information he needs to understand why he is struggling. He also needs to understand why so many complaints are being registered and, given the opportunity to change, hopefully, recover the respect and support of the department members.

Rationale for Rejecting the Alternate Solutions

A. Doing nothing will only result in more complaints if the poor behavior continues and will almost certainly result in losing a promising beginning leader. Simply put, this strategy is lose-lose strategy.

B. A tempting solution but it is best to hear both sides and seek a change that satisfies both parties (even if one party is a whole department).

Author's note: The result of the counseling session was that the young department head had received some "advice" from a close friend and former mentor. The advice was that when you become a supervisor the first thing you should do is "show them who is boss." This approach got him off to a bad start with his employees and was not his natural way of dealing with people. He settled down and became a very good supervisor.

LEADERSHIP = HEARTBURN

Best Solution: E—Building a positive relationship with the professors may eventually help moderate their resistance.

Rationale for Best Solution: Considering the other options, this is the only one that has any chance of reducing professor resistance and building a more positive college work environment and culture.

Rationale for Rejecting the Alternate Solutions

A. This option may facilitate a loss of respect from faculty and loss of support from the president. It may also lead to further turmoil.

B. This option would be punitive and lead to problems with those faculty members who were supportive of you.

C. This option would represent avoidance behavior and negative consequences may follow you to your new place of employment.

D. This option would lead to additional problems as the professors would appear to be intentionally isolated and then be able to garner support among other faculty members.

F. This may be perceived by faculty as the president trying to intentionally mislead the faculty to diffuse the situation and thereby reduce the power of the belligerent and uncooperative professors.

INSIDER INFORMATION

Best Solution: C—Have some private conversations with a couple of other board members that you trust about the issues of which you are aware.

Rationale for Best Solution: This is most likely the safest way to try and help the situation at the two-year school while hopefully not creating any problems or making life miserable for those working at the institution. While talking to a couple of other board members privately, you can discuss the problems of which you are aware without discussing the names of those who brought them to your attention. Once these board members understand the precariousness of your position, then they might be motivated to ask some questions and look into the situation.

Rationale for Rejecting the Alternate Solutions

A. This would be the easiest option, but doing nothing would be unethical since, as a board member, you are sworn to always act in the best interests of the institution.

B. This would definitely place the problems at the forefront and everyone will be made aware, but the executive head can (and most likely will based on what everyone knows) make lives miserable for the faculty and staff.

D. This is not a bad idea, but what if your colleagues talk and your students (who work at the two-year institution) will know that you are spreading the information in which they confided in you?

TASTY TREATS?

Best Solution: A—Write a note of apology to the provost and send an appropriate gift as reparation.

Rationale for Best Solution: A trying evening brought an accidental misstep. Correct it with a sincere apology and an edible gift to replace those taken at the behest of the president.

Rationale for Rejecting the Alternate Solutions

B. If needed this might be a possibility, but it is always better to attempt to find solutions on your own.

C. Some things require this action. However, it is not a good first step toward a resolution of the problem.

D. If needed this might be a possibility, but it is always better to attempt to find solutions on your own.

Author's note: I wrote a note of apology to the provost and told him that I must have lost my mind at the reception. The experience entertaining our guests, the unzipped zipper, the New Guinea rats, and the job offer that would not go away must have led to my momentary theft of the goodies. Additionally, I had the bakery prepare a pizza-sized monogrammed chocolate chip cookie for his office in reparation. He came to my office, accepted my apology, and named me assistant vice president reporting to him. I enjoyed working for this wonderful man until his retirement as president of the university. Every year I was his assistant, he ensured that I learned as much as possible about the institutional budget, from development to monitoring; that I participated and led regional accreditation activities at both the institutional and the regional levels; that I reviewed annually the pay of every single employee at the university in terms of fairness; that I represented the university on city and state committees as well as national conferences; that I understood the relationships and importance of both political and "friends of the University." Moreover, the most important gift that I received from him was that the most significant role of a college administer is to serve as the "moral compass of the institution." Every decision must be made on behalf of the institution and represent high ethical standards.

A WORD TO THE WISE

Best Solution: D—Go see the new department head and tell him you had no intention to interfere with his department in any way and that you will visit less often and make the visits shorter.

Rationale for Best Solution: While the action of the new department head is irritating, following the admonition of your supervisor to "make things right" for the sake of smooth functioning of the department is the best course of action.

Rationale for Rejecting the Alternate Solutions

A. Tempting but counterproductive.
B. This too is tempting but fails to address your supervisor's admonition.
C. Tempting but counterproductive.

INTERNATIONAL STUDENT DILEMMA

Best Solution: B—Enforce the rule.

Rationale for Best Solution: It would be unfair to others if an exception was made. Furthermore, legal issues might be raised by others.

Rationale for Rejecting the Alternate Solutions

A. Exceptions almost universally invite criticism for unfair treatment, if not outright favoritism.
C. As an "after-the-fact" solution, if deemed appropriate, this might be considered but changing rules in the throes of a crisis is bad practice unless the rule is deemed faulty as written.
D. The too might be a good after-the-fact solution. It might provide some comfort for the family.

CLEARING THE AIR

Best Solution: D—Explain the realities of sexual harassment in the current climate while assuring her of my respect for her work.

Rationale for Best Solution: This approach addresses both important issues, the potential for physical contact to be viewed negatively and then uplifts her by praising her work.

Rationale for Rejecting the Alternate Solutions

A. This addresses part but not all of the issues raised.
B. This addresses part but not all of the issues raised.
C. This is straightforward and may be what you think but does nothing to resolve the issue.

Author's note: Not sure it worked. She never was too happy with me regardless of my explanation.

A DAY'S PAY FOR A DAY'S WORK

Best Solution: B—Do not make the undeserved change in title.
Rationale for Best Solution: If the work she performs is that of a secretary, she does not warrant a pay increase.

Rationale for Rejecting the Alternate Solutions

A. Assigning a position on an improper basis is tantamount to showing favoritism.
C. What others do may at times impact your decisions but this decision is best made unilaterally.
D. This may be necessary at some point but is not a good first step.

Author's note: Since other administrators did make changes, my decision was not popular.

WORKING IT OUT

Best Solution: D—Write out a strongly written request to your supervisor to do the following: Approve an immediate exception to the work-from-home policy for this employee for the duration of her recuperation. This would be welcome to the employee because of her indicated desire to work from home and her lack of accumulated sick leave. Additionally, you should try hard to convince your supervisor of the importance of this solution. This should be done in person, not just by a written memorandum or email.

Rationale for Best Solution: This response has the best chance for success. It shows your supervisor that you have considered all of the ramifications of missing deadlines and that although he or she may be your superior that does not mean he or she understands the best way to work out the details. It also sends a strong message to your employees that you are not only serious about successfully meeting goals, but that you have also considered what is in their individual best interests as well. (In this case, this was a competent, well-respected employee and this solution was well received by her and her coworkers.)

Rationale for Rejecting the Alternate Solutions

A. It is always best to shoulder your own responsibilities. However, making the supervisor aware is a good step.
B. Wishful thinking/hoping usually ends badly and will not solve the problem.
C. Taking pills may calm your nerves but will not solve the problem.
E. A possible solution but one that goes against current policy.
F. If the other employees are capable of the work and if the overtime is approvable, this might be a solution but requires others to carry out her tasks.

APPENDIX A

SMALL GROUP CARDS

(Cut out individual letters and laminate for class use)

A	B
C	D
E	F

APPENDIX B

LEADER ACUMEN INTERPRETATION CHART

When reviewing your Self/Circle graph, keep in mind that there can be four outcomes for each of the five skillsets, as well as your total Leader Acumen score. Begin by considering your total score; then, move to your category of greatest relative weakness. Remember, a strength overused can become a liability.

Leader Acumen Self/Circle Assessment Matrix*	
High Self/High Circle *Most Desirable Orientation* *Strong in category and strong Self/Circle congruence suggests that Leadership Orientation is well developed and recognized.* *Skill enhancement is advisable for continued success.*	**Low Self/High Circle** *A Problematic Orientation* *(Preferred over a High Self/Low Circle orientation)* *Low Self scores and high Circle scores indicate a Leadership Orientation lacking in leader self-confidence.* *Leader growth is needed although the Circle has confidence in the leader.*
High Self/Low Circle *A Problematic Orientation* *Leadership Potential for Egocentric/Narcissistic Orientation* *Weak Circle congruence suggests a need for leader growth and development of the Leader–Circle relationship.* *Without growth derailment is likely.*	**Low Self/Low Circle** *Least Desirable Orientation* *Orientation with most room for growth.* *Though there may be congruence between the Self and Circle scores in this orientation, this Leadership orientation suggests a need for leader growth and development of the Leader–Circle relationship focused on success.*

* The Self and Circle scores, as well as congruence of the Self and Circle scores, vary along a spectrum from low to high. For each scenario, the Authors' Choices are typical of high Self/high Circle responses. This matrix represents the most likely outcomes and orientations.

APPENDIX C

LEADERSHIP ORIENTATION

Being perceived as and feeling individually that you are competent is vital to a leader's success. To this end, higher education leaders, like competent leaders in all fields, impact the perceptions of others by the way they behave/act/speak. Those behaviors/acts/utterances exemplify/personify the leader's level of competence to organizational members and constituents. But how can a leader gain insight or come to understand how he or she is perceived? One way is to gain such insight/understanding into how he or she is perceived is through a 360-evaluative feedback.

In combination with that feedback, it is vital that a leader individually be consistently reflective personally and professionally. That reflective process allows a leader to understand who he or she is and what he or she stands for as a leader and defines his or her leadership competence. That competence is one characteristic that tends to set him or her apart as a leader; to give him or her discernibility. And, competence is often the key to both long-term and short-term success as a leader.

A list of characteristics often associated with effective leadership in higher education is provided in the following table. Rate each of the following items on a scale of 1 to 10 (with 1 being lowest importance and 10 being highest importance) in relation to the item's importance in the displaying leadership competence. A scoring rubric is provided in Appendix D.

1	Establish principles of treating people	1	2	3	4	5	6	7	8	9	10
2	Foster collaboration	1	2	3	4	5	6	7	8	9	10
3	Seek opportunities to make changes	1	2	3	4	5	6	7	8	9	10
4	Envision the future with a unique image	1	2	3	4	5	6	7	8	9	10
5	Keep hope and determination alive	1	2	3	4	5	6	7	8	9	10
6	Experiment and take risks	1	2	3	4	5	6	7	8	9	10
7	Set standards of excellence	1	2	3	4	5	6	7	8	9	10

8	Get people to see exciting possibilities	1	2	3	4	5	6	7	8	9	10
9	Recognize individuals' contributions	1	2	3	4	5	6	7	8	9	10
10	Build team spirit	1	2	3	4	5	6	7	8	9	10
11	Breathe life into the (organizational) vision	1	2	3	4	5	6	7	8	9	10
12	Share rewards within the team	1	2	3	4	5	6	7	8	9	10
13	Actively involve others	1	2	3	4	5	6	7	8	9	10
14	Create opportunities for success	1	2	3	4	5	6	7	8	9	10
15	Accept mistakes, disappointments, and failures as opportunities to learn	1	2	3	4	5	6	7	8	9	10

The table is based on the work of Simon Black.

Enter your rating for each of the following items and in the scoring rubric for Leadership Orientation.

1 _____   2 _____   3 _____   4 _____   5 _____

6 _____   7 _____   8 _____   9 _____   10 _____

11 _____   12 _____   13 _____   14 _____   15 _____

Categories are based on the work of Simon Black.[1]

Scoring: Models the way = sum items 1, 7, and 14

_____ + _____ + _____ = _____
  1   7   14   Models the way total score

Inspire a shared vision = sum items 4, 8, and 11

_____ + _____ + _____ = _____
  4   8   11   Inspire a shared vision total score

Challenge the process = sum items 3, 6, and 15

_____ + _____ + _____ = _____
  3   6   15   Challenge the process total score

Enable others to act = sum items 2, 10, and 13

_____ + _____ + _____ = _____
  2   10   13   Enable others to act total score

Encourage the heart = sum items 5, 9, and 12

_____ + _____ + _____ = _____
  5   9   12   Encourage the heart total score

Interpretation: The scores represent your emphasis of a given orientation as a higher education leader. The higher the score, the more prominent that orientation emphasis is likely to be in your leadership activities.

APPENDIX D

FUN AT WORK?

Happiness is a highly individualized and internalized feeling both personally and professionally. While for the purposes of discussion, personal and professional happiness can be separated, the two often carryover and impact each other. Still, being happy in our personal lives does not guarantee happiness in our professional lives nor does the opposite apply.

Beyond whatever carryover exists, a leader has minimal opportunities to impact the personal happiness of organizational members. Conversely, there are things a leader can do to increase potential professional happiness.

Rate each of the following items on a scale of 1 to 10 (with 1 being lowest importance and 10 being highest importance) in relation to the items' importance in promoting organizational members professional happiness. A scoring rubric is provided.

A	Encourage organizational members to offer praise when accomplishments are achieved	1	2	3	4	5	6	7	8	9	10
B	Provide access to high-quality training and professional growth opportunities	1	2	3	4	5	6	7	8	9	10
C	At appropriate times, encourage staff members to take earned time off	1	2	3	4	5	6	7	8	9	10
D	Display energy and enthusiasm in working with organizational members	1	2	3	4	5	6	7	8	9	10
E	Ensure that pay and benefits are competitive, fair, equal for equal work, and maximized	1	2	3	4	5	6	7	8	9	10
F	Be cordial and friendly	1	2	3	4	5	6	7	8	9	10
G	Provide organizational members opportunities for decision-making discretion (Porath et al., 2012)	1	2	3	4	5	6	7	8	9	10

H	Offer to mentor aspiring leaders	1	2	3	4	5	6	7	8	9	10
I	Provide feedback about performance (Porath et. al., 2012)	1	2	3	4	5	6	7	8	9	10
J	Have and share an optimistic outlook as a leader.	1	2	3	4	5	6	7	8	9	10
K	Provide equal access to opportunities for promotion.	1	2	3	4	5	6	7	8	9	10
L	Deflect praise for successes to the responsible organizational members.	1	2	3	4	5	6	7	8	9	10

Scoring: Egocentric = sum items D, F, H, and J

$$\underline{\hspace{1cm}} + \underline{\hspace{1cm}} + \underline{\hspace{1cm}} + \underline{\hspace{1cm}} = \underline{\hspace{3cm}}$$

D　　F　　H　　J　　total Egocentric score

People-oriented = sum items A, C, E, and L

$$\underline{\hspace{1cm}} + \underline{\hspace{1cm}} + \underline{\hspace{1cm}} + \underline{\hspace{1cm}} = \underline{\hspace{3cm}}$$

A　　C　　E　　L　　total People-oriented score

Task-oriented = sum items B, G, I, and K

$$\underline{\hspace{1cm}} + \underline{\hspace{1cm}} + \underline{\hspace{1cm}} + \underline{\hspace{1cm}} = \underline{\hspace{3cm}}$$

B　　G　　I　　K　　total Task-oriented score

Interpretation: The scores represent your tendencies toward behaviors that promote organizational members' professional happiness. The higher the score, the more prominent this orientation is likely to be in your leadership activities. Maximum score for each category is 40.

BACKGROUND

Professional satisfaction/happiness has been shown to be related to worker performance. Therefore, incorporating those behaviors in a leader's repertoire of behaviors enhances the probability of worker satisfaction/happiness and organizational productivity.

Kerns, C. D. (2008). "Putting Performance and Happiness Together in the Workplace." *Graziado Business Review*, *1*(1). Retrieved October 15, 2016 from http://gbr.pepperdine.edu/2010/08/putting-performance-and-happiness-together-in-the-workplace/.

Leader to Leader. (2012). "The Importance of Happiness in the Workplace." 2012 (63), 62–63. doi:10.1002/ltl.20012.

Porath, C., Spreitzer, G., Gibson, C., and Garnett, F. G. (2012). "Thriving at Work: Toward Its Measurement, Construct Validation, and Theoretical Refinement." *Journal of Organizational Behavior*, *33*(2), 250–275. doi:10.1002/job.756.

APPENDIX E

SELF-KNOWLEDGE

Warren Bennis (2002), well-known author and leadership expert, says of leaders, "The ruling quality of leaders, adaptive capacity, is what allows true leaders to make the nimble decisions that bring success. Adaptive capacity is also what allows some people to transcend the setbacks and losses that come with age and to reinvent themselves again and again."[3]

Bennis's notion of adaptive capacity can be viewed as an applied amalgamation of the personality traits espoused in the five-factor model of personality. McCrea and John (1992) in describing the five-factor model held that there are "five basic dimensions: Extraversion, Agreeableness, Conscientiousness, Neuroticism, and Openness to Experience."[4] Neuroticism, in this instance, can be further defined as emotional stability.

1. Read each item carefully.
2. Select the answer that best describes how often you engage in the behavior described: (A) Always, (B) Often, (C) Occasionally, (D) Seldom, or (E) Never.
3. CIRCLE the letter (A, B, C, D, or E) of the answer you select.

A scoring rubric is provided in the Authors' Options section at the end of the chapter.

Item #	Item	Always	Often	Occasionally	Seldom	Never
A	I like to join multiple groups/ organizations	A	B	C	D	E
B	I consider myself imaginative in my approach tasks	A	B	C	D	E
C	I am even-tempered	A	B	C	D	E
D	I am hardworking	A	B	C	D	E
E	I am generally good-natured	A	B	C	D	E

Item #	Item	Always	Often	Occasionally	Seldom	Never
F	I am comfortable personally and professionally	A	B	C	D	E
G	I have a strong sense of curiosity	A	B	C	D	E
H	I am punctual	A	B	C	D	E
I	I tend to be forgiving of mistakes	A	B	C	D	E
J	I remain calm in most situations	A	B	C	D	E
K	I am active physically and mentally	A	B	C	D	E
L	I seek new approaches	A	B	C	D	E
M	I am trusting of others	A	B	C	D	E
N	I am highly verbal	A	B	C	D	E
O	I am well organized	A	B	C	D	E

BACKGROUND

The five-factor model of personality has been shown to be related to a variety of factors that contribute to leadership success such as job satisfaction (Judge, Heller, and Mount, 2002), life satisfaction (DeNeve and Cooper, 1998), organization citizenship (Chiaburu et al., 2011), and work environment (Ruth, 2016). Aspects of the model, specifically extraversion and agreeableness, have been shown to be positively related to transformational leadership (Judge and Bono, 2000).

Chiaburu, D. S., Oh, I., Berry, C. M., Li, N., and Gardner, R. G. (2011). "The Five-Factor Model of Personality Traits and Organizational Citizenship Behaviors: A Meta-Analysis." *The Journal of Applied Psychology*, *96*(6), 1140–1166. doi:10.1037/a0024004.

DeNeve, K. M. and Cooper, H. (1998). "The Happy Personality: A Meta-Analysis of 137 Personality Traits and Subjective Well-Being." *Psychological Bulletin*, *124*(2), 197.

Judge, T. A. and Bono, J. E. (2000). "Five-Factor Model of Personality and Transformational Leadership." *Journal of Applied Psychology*, *85*(5), 751–765. doi:10.1037/0021–9010.85.5.751.

Judge, T. A., Heller, D., and Mount, M. K. (2002). "Five-Factor Model of Personality and Job Satisfaction: A Meta-Analysis." *Journal of Applied Psychology*, *87*(3), 530–541. doi:10.1037/0021–9010.87.3.530.

Ruth, J. A. (2016). "An examination of the impact of the big five personality traits and work environment on the leadership behaviors of millennial generation employees." *Dissertation Abstracts International Section A, 76.*

SELF-KNOWLEDGE

Item #	Item	Always	Often	Occasionally	Seldom	Never
1	I like to join multiple groups/organizations	A	B	C	D	E
2	I consider myself imaginative in my approach tasks	A	B	C	D	E

Item #	Item	Always	Often	Occasionally	Seldom	Never
3	I am even-tempered	A	B	C	D	E
4	I am hardworking	A	B	C	D	E
5	I am generally good-natured	A	B	C	D	E
6	I am comfortable personally and professionally	A	B	C	D	E
7	I have a strong sense of curiosity	A	B	C	D	E
8	I am punctual	A	B	C	D	E
9	I tend to be forgiving of mistakes	A	B	C	D	E
10	I remain calm in most situations	A	B	C	D	E
11	I am active physically and mentally	A	B	C	D	E
12	I seek new approaches	A	B	C	D	E
13	I am trusting of others	A	B	C	D	E
14	I am highly verbal	A	B	C	D	E
15	I am well organized	A	B	C	D	E

*Scale items are based on the "Examples of Adjectives, Q-Sort Items, and Questionnaire Scales Defining the Five Factors" (McRae and John, 1992, pp. 178–179).

Sources: Bennis, W. G. (2004). "The Seven Ages of the Leader." *Harvard Business Review*, *82*(1), 46.

McCrae, R. R. and John, O. P. (1992). "An Introduction to the Five-Factor Model and Its Applications." *Journal of Personality*, *60*(2), 175–215.

SCORING

For the letter selected for each item give yourself the following points. Then total the scores for each category.

A = 5   B = 4   C = 3   D = 2   E = 1

				Total
1. Extraversion	1__	11__	14__	(____)
2. Agreeableness	5__	9__	13__	(____)
3. Conscientiousness	4__	8__	15__	(____)
4. Neuroticism (emotional stability)	3__	6__	10__	(____)
5. Openness to experience	2__	7__	12__	(____)

INTERPRETATION

The wide acceptance of the five-factor model and the extensive research indicating the relationship of the model's factors to leadership and life success make it essential that leaders understand their personality tendencies and dispositions. The results of this scale indicate your self-perception in relation to the aspects the five-factor model. A higher score in a given area indicates that your personality tends to reflect characteristics of that factor.

APPENDIX F

ACTIVITIES TO IMPROVE YOUR LEADER ACUMEN

Now is a good time to reflect on the navigational analysis. Let us consider that you are the driver for a chartered bus with thirty-five travelers to a landmark tourist adventure 600 miles away. You have made many trips over your life that were 600 miles or longer, but perhaps you have never been to this particular destination. Maybe some of those on the bus are older than you are and have driven longer. Perhaps, even, some of them have been to the destination at hand on a previous occasion. Prior to embarking on the trip, you have several options in preparation for the trip.

Regardless of how you chose to prepare, each of your travelers has his or her own expectations regarding the trip. Some may wish you would drive faster, others might wish you would have taken the more leisurely scenic route. Still others may question the detours, pit stops, and even announcements you make. All of these factors (and many others) would inform their feedback on your performance as a driver.

After returning from your destination and having a little time to reflect on the trip, you too might consider different decisions you would make if you had the chance to "drive the bus again." Your own reflections as well as the passenger's feedback would certainly leave an imprint. How strong an imprint might depend on the degree of congruence between your perception of the trip and theirs?

In order to improve the next trip (and not to imply that this one was a bad one), the driver needs to be reflective, ask for feedback, and plan for the future. This planning (for improvement) could include a myriad of things from using a more updated map (or Global Positioning System [GPS]) to planning to take the trip at a better time of year. It will include both study and action.

The same planning for improvement, study, and action is true with *Leader Acumen*. The scenarios in the field book are given to help the leader consider the myriad of solutions to different problems and to become more effective and efficient at resolving them. Whether in a group setting with the rich dialogue, discourse, and reflective dynamics that setting generates or considered individually, study leading to action will be the best teacher and provide a clear/direct route to success in increasing your *Leader Acumen.*

As the leader becomes aware of and chooses the construct or skillset (Credibility, Competence, Inspiration, Vision, or Emotional Intelligence) he or she would most like to improve, along with the exercises in the book, the following activities are recommended. For the best results, these activities should be planned and acted upon over a period of not less than six months.

To improve your CREDIBILITY, while working through the book scenarios, as odd as it may seem, write an article or research paper for publication to share your experiences and expertise. This is *not* a one-week assignment. You should set aside (at a minimum) weekly time to work on the article or paper; organizing, researching, and writing the article or paper. This will not just be for the sake of obtaining facts and information, but it will also be for the purpose of presenting them. How you present yourself in your writing is a huge part of your credibility.

If you rush through and/or are sloppy, you leave a distinctly poor impression with the reader (think emails, memoranda, and even handwritten notes). As a leader, in any written correspondence, if you give the facts and figures without ensuring they are valid, reliable, and in fact real, again, you lose credibility. As you are preparing your paper, work to triangulate (using multiple data sources) to ensure your credibility. A second option would be to undertake case study readings about historical or contemporary figures you admire and believe to be credible and reflect on what about that individual/ those individuals made them credible. These case studies could also be incorporated into your article or research paper.

To improve your COMPETENCE, while working through the book scenarios, align yourself with a mentor in your field of leadership and meet with him or her regularly. Try to find opportunities not only to interact with this person on an informal basis, but more importantly find opportunities to "shadow" this person. Write down a list of questions to ask about how he or she arrived at a specific solution or why they took a certain position. Take the time to discuss with your mentor other solutions that he or she (or you) might have considered. Talk to this person about typical problems/issues they encounter and how they approach resolving those problems/issues. Spend as much time talking about the why as the what, how, and about the timing of their decisions. Do not be timid when asking about technical matters. Technical matters form the basis of what people are to accomplish.

To improve your ABILITY TO INSPIRE OTHERS, while working through the book scenarios, join a speaker's bureau. Conversely, become a coach/sponsor/leader for a children's athletic, drama, music, or scout group. You might rather choose to join adult groups such as a neighborhood watch, owners' association, or civic group such as Rotary or Lions where you would have the opportunity to lead by your words and actions.

As a member of a speakers' group, seek opportunities to present motivational/inspirational messages regularly. The same is true if you choose to become a volunteer coach/sponsor/leader of children's groups. Be sure that you give motivational pitches regularly to the children. With adults, volunteer to lead or participate in group activities. Being actively involved in the suggested activities should present ample opportunities to both observe and be a part of inspirational activities and should have a corresponding positive impact on your overall ability in this area.

To improve your VISION, while working through the book scenarios, embark on a personal improvement plan. This can be anything from a physical, spiritual, mental, or emotional area of your life. This idea is to choose an area for self-improvement and then to map out a six-month plan to reach a specific goal. As Covey would say, "Begin with the end in mind."[1] Once you have created the plan, and make it very detailed and specific, enact the plan. At the end of each month, evaluate/reflect on your progress and then adjust your plan accordingly. Or, as an alternative strategy, plan an event or series of events for your family or other group with which you are associated. Be sure to engage family or group members in the planning processes to produce a shared vision regarding each event. The personal plan or the planning of events should engage you actively in the give and take of reaching a personal decision that impacts your individual plan (or the consensus) that is needed for visionary action.

To improve your EMOTIONAL INTELLIGENCE/SOFT SKILLS, while working through the book scenarios, commit yourself to involvement with a charitable, civic, school, religious, or other worthwhile organization that is not a part of your work. Focus your energies not only on the betterment of the cause/organization but also specifically on the people affiliated with the cause/organization. Be intentional in your desire to encourage, support, and embolden them. Or, as an alternative strategy, volunteer to assist in projects sponsored by local civic groups that involve working with people in need or volunteer to work in an appropriate capacity at a hospital or nursing home, or to assist youth groups in your community. The emotional impact of serving others selflessly should provide opportunities for growth in your emotional intelligence.

The combination of intense review of SJTs along with the activities, as briefly described earlier, over a period of time will ensure growth in your chosen *Leader Acumen* skillset. Not only will your skillset scores improve, but more importantly, your leadership capacity will improve. Your road to success as a leader will be like an up-to-date GPS with all the latest features, newest maps, and best route guidance available.

NOTES

SITUATIONAL JUDGMENT TESTS

1. Wanda S. Maulding Green and Edward E. Leonard. *Improving Your Leadership Intelligence: A Field Book for K–12 Leaders*. (Lanham, MD: Rowman & Littlefield, 2016).

2. Warren G. Bennis and Robert Thomas. *Geeks and Geezers: How Era, Values, and Defining Moments Shape Leaders*. (Boston, MA: Harvard Business School Publishing, 2002).

3. Ibid.

4. Warren G. Bennis. "The seven ages of the leader." *Harvard Business Review*, 82(1), 46 (2004).

5. Cisco's John Chambers on the digital era (2016). Retrieved from http://www.mckinsey.com/industries/high-tech/our-insights/ciscosjohn-chambers-on-the-digital-era.

6. MaryUhl-Bien and MichaelArena. "Leadership for organizational adaptability: A theoretical synthesis and integrative framework." *The Leadership Quarterly*, 29(1), 89–104 (2018). https://doi-org.lynx.lib.usm.edu/10.1016/j.leaqua.2017.12.009.

7. M. Uhl-Bien & M. Arena. Leadership for organizational adaptability: A theoretical synthesis and integrative framework. *The Leadership Quarterly*, 29(1), 89–104 (2018). https://doi-org.lynx.lib.usm.edu/10.1016/j.leaqua.2017.12.009

8. Catherine Bond Hill. Welcoming Remarks. 2010. Retrieved from https://www.vassar.edu/remarks/convocation/2010b/president-hill.html.

9. Wanda S. Maulding Green and Edward E. Leonard. *Leadership Intelligence: Navigating to Your True North*. (Lanham, MD: Rowman & Littlefield, 2016).

* *Disclaimer: At the end of the book are the author's recommended solutions, rationale, and reasoning for rejection of alternative solutions. These recommendations are in no way intended to supersede work policy or act as legal advice to the learner. If encountering similar situations, you should consult with proper authorities and/or act as you deem appropriate based on your own judgment. The Situational Judgement Test (SJT) scenarios included are based on actual situa-*

tions encountered by the authors including the solutions they enacted at the time and place of the circumstance and may or may not be appropriate today individually or in your place of work.

10. Michael McDaniel and Deborah Whetzel. "Situational Judgement Tests." Lecture, IP-MAAC Workshop, June 20, 2005.

11. Michael McDaniel, Frederick Morgeson, Elizabeth Finnigan, and Michael Campion. "Use of situational judgment tests to predict job performance: A clarification of the literature." *Journal of Applied Psychology, 84*(4), 730–740 (2001).

CHAPTER 1

1. Christopher Marquis and Andras Tilcsik. "Imprinting: Toward a multilevel theory." *The Academy of Management Annals*, 7(1), 195–245 (2013).

CHAPTER 3

1. Christopher Marquis and Andras Tilcsik. "Imprinting: Toward a multilevel theory." *The Academy of Management Annals*, 7(1), 195–245 (2013).

CHAPTER 5

1. Christopher Marquis and Andras Tilcsik. "Imprinting: Toward a multilevel theory." *The Academy of Management Annals*, 7(1), 195–245 (2013).

2. Wanda S. Maulding Green and Edward E. Leonard, *Leadership Intelligence: Navigating to Your True North* (Lanham, MD: Rowman & Littlefield, 2016).

CHAPTER 7

1. Christopher Marquis and Andras Tilcsik. "Imprinting: Toward a multilevel theory." *The Academy of Management Annals*, 7(1), 195–245 (2013).

2. Wanda S. Maulding Green and Edward E. Leonard, *Leadership Intelligence: Navigating to Your True North* (Lanham, MD: Rowman & Littlefield, 2016).

CHAPTER 9

1. Christopher Marquis and Andras Tilcsik. "Imprinting: Toward a multilevel theory." *The Academy of Management Annals*, 7(1), 195–245 (2013).

2. Wanda S. Maulding Green and Edward E. Leonard, *Leadership Intelligence: Navigating to Your True North* (Lanham, MD: Rowman & Littlefield, 2016).

APPENDIX C

1. Simon A. Black, "Qualities of Effective Leadership in Higher Education," *Open Journal of Leadership* 4(2) (2015): 54–66. Retrieved October 15, 2016 from http://file.scirp.org/Html/2-233 0076_57195.htm.

APPENDIX E

1. Warren G. Bennis, "The Seven Ages of the Leader," *Harvard Business Review* 82(1) (January 2004): 46.

2. Robert R. McCrae and Oliver P. John, "An Introduction to the Five-Factor Model and Its Applications," *Journal of Personality* 60(2) (June 1992): 175–215.

APPENDIX F

1. Covey, S. (1989). The seven habits of highly effective people : Restoring the character ethic : 7 habits of highly effective people. New York: Simon & Schuster.

ABOUT THE AUTHORS

Wanda S. Maulding Green is an educational leadership faculty member at the University of South Alabama and has served in leadership roles in both K–12 and higher education. She is the coauthor of the book, *Leadership Intelligence: Navigating to Your True North.*

Edward E. Leonard is a retired school superintendent and higher education administrator. He currently teaches leadership courses at the University of South Alabama and is the coauthor of the book, *Leadership Intelligence: Navigating to Your True North.*

ABOUT THE CONTRIBUTORS

M. Wayne Davis, BS, MA, had a fifty-two-year career as a university financial administrator and is now retired. He began his career as a student employee in the Payroll Department at the University of Alabama and spent thirty-six years at the University of South Alabama, serving as the vice president for financial affairs for the past twenty-four years at that institution.

Dr. Susan Gordon-Hickey is an associate professor of audiology and currently serves as an associate dean at her institution. She is a fellow of the American Academy of Audiology and a member of the Editorial Board of the *American Auditory Societies Ear and Hearing Journal*.

Dr. Kelly Osterbind is a university registrar with over ten years of experience at two different institutions. She has a doctorate in educational leadership and enthusiastically mentors young leaders in her field. Kelly is also an active volunteer in her local community.

Dr. Jalynn Roberts is the director of research support at William Carey University, MS, USA. He teaches statistics to students in math, nursing, and education. He also serves as methodologist and statistician on student dissertation committees and faculty research projects.

Dr. Bob Shearer is a mediator, arbitrator, and consultant. Upon retiring from the University of South Alabama in 2015, he was named professor emeritus in the Mitchell College of Business, AL, USA. Previously, he had held the positions of special assistant to presidents at USA and at Christopher Newport University in Newport News, VA. He also served as vice president for planning and assessment at Brevard (FL) Community College.

Dr. Ronald Styron is currently serving on the leadership faculty at the University of South Alabama. He has served in various roles over the past forty years including K–12 teacher, K–12 administrator, university professor, and university administrator. He most recently served as director of a quality enhancement plan with the purpose of integrating an instructional strategy called team-based learning in multiple disciplines across a university campus.

Dr. Margaret Sullivan is currently employed as the associate vice chancellor of academic affairs in a large private institution. Prior to this she served as chancellor of University of South Florida, St. Petersburg. She has had extensive leadership experience in both private and public universities. Additionally, she has served as an accreditation consultant and has assisted more than 200 institutions and university systems in the southeastern United States.

Dr. Jeral Williams is a retired sports psychologist and university vice president. He continues to work with golf athletes at the collegiate level and as a mentor for many, both on and off the field. He is also the author of the book *Being a Proverbial Student: Getting a Degree vs. Getting an Education.*